Answers to Everyday Questions 1

<High-beginning>

身近な不思議を英語で学ぶ

＜初級＞

JN004189

Arnold Arao
Kei Mihara
Yoshinori Miwa
Hiroshi Kimura

NAN'UN-DO

Answers to Everyday Questions 1
<High-beginning>

© Copyright 2024
by
Arnold Arao
Kei Mihara
Yoshinori Miwa
Hiroshi Kimura

All rights Reserved
No part of this book may be reproduced in any form without
permission from the authors and Nan'un-do Co., Ltd.

Download Audio
音声ファイル
無料 DL
のご案内

このテキストの音声を無料で視聴（ストリーミング）・ダウンロードできます。自習用音声としてご活用ください。
以下のサイトにアクセスしてテキスト番号で検索してください。

https://nanun-do.com　テキスト番号 [**512198**]

※ 無線 LAN（WiFi）に接続してのご利用を推奨いたします。

※ 音声ダウンロードは Zip ファイルでの提供になります。
お使いの機器によっては別途ソフトウェア（アプリケーション）の導入が必要となります。

Read by

Shizuka Anderson
Ryan Drees

※ Answers to Everyday Questions 1 音声ダウンロードページは以下の QR コードからもご利用になれます。

はじめに

私たちの身の回りには不思議なことが溢れています。不思議な事象について、「なぜ？」と疑問を抱くことがあるでしょう。そこから不思議の扉が開き、思いがけない楽しい知識の冒険が始まるのです。ふと生じる「なぜ？」に耳を傾け、身近にある不思議な事象を楽しみながら考えてみましょう。

「なぜ？」と問う好奇心を持つことで、普段気づかないことに気づくことができます。好奇心は、学びたいという欲求の源泉で、知りたいと思うことの原動力なのです。それは勉強の楽しさを育むワクワクする芽で、大事に育てたいものです。

本書では、私たちの日常の暮らしの中で不思議と思う、素朴な疑問を学びます。たとえば、「曜日の名前の由来は？」「日常会話で使われる野球用語は？」「赤色で気持ちはハッピー」「爆発的に語彙を増やした劇作家」などなど、身近にある不思議に目を向けて考えることは、知的好奇心を刺激し、さらに、様々な社会的・文化的事象に目を向けるきっかけになります。身近な不思議は意外とたくさんあります。そこで、学生にとって、できるだけ興味深く、おもしろい 15 のトピックを選びました。

本書は英語の基本をしっかり固め、知識や技能だけでなく、「考える」英語力を身につけることを目的とした、初級レベルの英語総合教材です。「考える」英語力を養うため、主体性や思考力などを多面的に問う効果的に配置された練習問題を解くことで、リーディング、リスニング、ライティングの力を無理なく、バランスよく伸ばすことができます。

本書の特長

1. 語彙をチェックすることで、語彙力を増強
2. 180 語程度のエッセイをスキミング、スキャニングして、リーディング力を強化
3. 50 語程度の会話を聞くことで、リスニング力をアップ
4. 60 語程度の空所補充問題をこなし、表現力を定着
5. 文法問題を解くことで、文法力をマスター
6. 英作文を書くことで、ライティング力を習得

本書を通じて、「なぜ？」という好奇心を呼び起こしつつ、英語力の涵養に役立てば、筆者にとってこれに勝る喜びはありません。

2024 年 1 月
著者一同

本書の構成と使い方

Warm-up Questions
質問に英語で答えます。

1 Vocabulary

各ユニットの Reading に出てくる単語を、空所に入れて英文を完成します。

2 Reading

エッセイを読んで、内容を理解します。

A True or False

英文が本文の内容に合っていれば T (True)、間違っていれば F (False) を選びます。

B Skimming and Scanning

本文の内容について、最も適切な答えや語句を (A) ～ (C) から選びます。

3 Conversation

A Listen and Write

会話を聞いて空所に単語を書きます。

B Listen and Choose

質問を聞いて空所に単語を書き、最も適切な答えを (A) ～ (C) から選びます。

4 Text Completion

文章を完成するため、空所に入れる最も適切な語句や文を (A) ～ (C) から選びます。

5 Grammar

指示に従って文法問題を解きます。

6 Composition

A 日本語に合うように (　　) 内の語句を正しく並べ替えます。
B 質問に対する応答文を (　　) 内の語句を使って自由に書きます。

Grammar Spotlight
各ユニットの文法・語法を確認します。

Contents

Unit 1
On What Day Does the Week Start?

▶ **present tense / past tense**

カレンダーでは何曜日から週が始まるのでしょうか。日曜日、月曜日、それとも…。実は国によって異なるのです。アメリカや日本は日曜日を始まりとしています。ビジネスのグローバル化が進むにつれ、世界で統一した週の始まりが必要かもしれません。

Warm-up Questions

次の質問に英語で答えなさい。

1. What did you do yesterday?
2. What is your favorite day of the week? Why?

1 Vocabulary

英文の空所に入れる最も適切な単語を語群より選び、(A)～(G)で答えなさい。

(A) common	(B) established	(C) globalization	(D) however
(E) include	(F) surprised	(G) weekends	

1. The oldest university in the world is the University of Bologna. It was _____ in 1088.
2. In most western countries, it is _____ for people to use a fork or spoon when they eat.
3. Many textbooks now _____ extra audio CDs or online learning materials.
4. Thanks to _____, we can now order products from all over the world.
5. English is a popular language for people to learn; _____, many people also study other languages.
6. I go to school on weekdays and work at my part-time job on _____.
7. We were _____ to hear that Mr. Owens, our history teacher, was leaving. We thought he would be teaching us next year.

2 Reading

02

In Japan, Canada, and the United States, as well as in many South American countries, Sunday is the first day of the week. These countries all use an old calendar, known as the Gregorian calendar. Many years ago, however, because of increasing globalization, many companies wanted to standardize the way they did business. And one way they did this was to create a common five-day work week.

So in 1971, the ISO (International Organization for Standardization) established Monday as the first day of the week. People worked five days, starting on Monday and finishing on Friday. These five days are called weekdays. Saturdays and Sundays were days of rest. These two days are called the weekend. Countries that follow the ISO calendar include Russia, New Zealand, and most European countries.

But if you travel to the Middle East, you might be surprised to find that in many countries there, the first day of the week is not Sunday or Monday. It's Saturday!

Notes **Gregorian calendar**「グレゴリオ暦」 **standardize**「統一する」 **ISO**「国際標準化機構」 **the Middle East**「中東」

Reading Comprehension

A True or False

次の英文が本文の内容と一致する場合は T、一致しない場合は F を選びなさい。

1. In the United States, the first day of the week is Sunday. **[T F]**

2. In many European countries, the first day of the week is Sunday. **[T F]**

3. In every country in the world, the week starts on either Sunday or Monday. **[T F]**

B Skimming and Scanning

本文の内容について、空所に入れる最も適切なものを (A) ～ (C) から選びなさい。

1. The letters ISO stand for _____.

(A) International Office of Standards

(B) International Organization for Standardization

(C) International Standardization Office

2. The ISO made changes to the calendar in _____.

(A) 1910 (B) 1971 (C) 2001

3. The reason why some countries changed their calendar was because _____.

(A) companies wanted a common schedule for all workers

(B) those countries disliked the old calendar

(C) workers wanted more days off from work

3 Conversation

A Listen and Write

03

次の会話を聞いて、(　　)に単語を書きなさい。

M: What a long week!

W: It sure was! I [1](　　　　　　) believe how much work we had to do.

M: Well, it took us all week, but we managed to [2](　　　　　　) everything. So TGIF!

W: TGIF? I'm sorry, but what does that mean?

M: It stands for Thank God It's Friday! It means that the weekend is here, and we can finally [3](　　　　　　).

W: Oh, did you forget? We [4](　　　　　　) to come in to work tomorrow, too.

Notes　**It sure was!**「そうだよね！」　**TGIF**「神様ありがとう、金曜日だ」　**stand for**「〜を表す」

B Listen and Choose

04

質問を聞いて、(　　)に単語を書き、最も適切な応答を(A)〜(C)から選びなさい。

1. (　　　　) (　　　　) the man (　　　　　)?

(A) Because he has not finished all of the work yet

(B) Because he is almost finished working today

(C) Because tomorrow is the weekend

2. (　　　　) (　　　　) the man and woman probably (　　　　　)?

(A) Thursday afternoon　　(B) Friday evening　　(C) Saturday morning

4 Text Completion

次の文章を読んで、空所に入れる最も適切なものを(A)〜(C)から選びなさい。

Many schools around the world __1__ a five-day schedule. Classes __2__ on Monday and finish on Friday. This may soon change, however, as many countries want to extend the school week to Saturdays. Most schools still want to reduce the hours students spend at school each day, but they want to add an extra day so that __3__.

1. (A) use　　(B) used　　(C) using

2. (A) begin　　(B) begins　　(C) began

3. (A) students can hang out more with their friends

(B) students can spend more time with their families

(C) students can still learn everything they need to learn

5 Grammar Check

A (　　) 内の動詞を過去形にして、文章を完成しなさい。

Dear diary,

Last week our class (do) [1]__________ group projects. First, we (choose) [2]__________ our topic. Then, we (go) [3]__________ to the library and (get) [4]__________ some information. We (find) [5]__________ a lot of interesting articles and (see) [6]__________ some great photos in many different magazines. We (speak) [7]__________ to the librarian about using the photos. She (say) [8]__________ that we could. In the afternoon, we all (meet) [9]__________ in the cafeteria to work on our projects. It (be) [10]__________ a really busy day for us.

B 空所に入れる動詞を語群より選び、適切な現在形にして英文を完成しなさい。

be	go	live	pick	study

1. The school bus always ______________ up the children here at 7 a.m.
2. Every morning, Charles wakes up early and ______________ for a walk.
3. Jimmy ______________ in his new apartment.
4. My mother ______________ from Germany. She was born in Berlin.
5. Sophia goes to the library every day and ______________ American history.

C (　　) 内の最も適切な単語を選び、英文を完成しなさい。

1. Brian (watch / watches / watched) a very funny movie on TV last night.
2. On weekends, Jennifer usually (go / goes / going) shopping at the supermarket.
3. We won't go camping unless it (stop / stops / stopped) raining.
4. Liz and Kevin (are / was / were) not at work yesterday.
5. My teacher always says that there (is / was / were) no royal road to learning. What does that mean?
6. Let's start as soon as Meg (get / gets / got) here.
7. My daughter (eat / eats / ate) her lunch and then went to the playground.

6 Composition

A 日本語を参考にして、(　　) 内の単語を正しく並べ替え、また [　　] ア～ウに単語を書いて、文章を完成しなさい。

Do you like to [ア][　　　　　　] at home on Sundays? Is [1](difficult / for / it / to / you) go to school on Mondays? Do you [2](forward / hanging / look / out / to) with your friends on Saturday? Many [3](plan / people / schedules / their / weekly) starting on Sunday, the [イ][　　　　　　] day of the week. But did you know that in some parts of the world, the week [ウ][　　　　　　] on Monday, or even Saturday?

日曜日に家で、くつろぐのは好きですか。月曜日に通学するのはつらいですか。土曜日に友だちと一緒に過ごすのを楽しみにしていますか。多くの人は、週の最初の日である日曜日から毎週のスケジュールを計画します。しかし、世界のいくつかの地域では、週が月曜日、あるいは土曜日に始まることさえあるのを知っていましたか。

Word Order:

1.

2.

3.

B 次の質問に、(　　) 内の語句を使って答えなさい。

1. What did you do last weekend?

(went to / we played)

2. Write about what you did yesterday. Use **Grammar Check A** (p.10) as an example.

(Dear diary, / Yesterday was … / First, … / Then, … / Next, … / After that, …)

Grammar Spotlight

▶現在時制

現在の動作や状態、一般的な事実等を表すとき、動詞の「現在形」を使います。

1. 現在の動作

We **play** soccer on Sundays.
Susan always **goes** to school by bicycle.
Nick often **travels** on business.

☞ always, often, usually, sometimes など、頻度の副詞をよく伴います。

2. 現在の状態

Liz **lives** in the suburbs of Seattle.
I **like** to take landscape photos as a hobby.

3. 一般的な事実、ことわざ

Water **freezes** at zero degrees Celsius.
The early bird **catches** the worm.

▶過去時制

過去の動作や状態、事実について表すとき、動詞の「過去形」を使います。

1. 過去の動作

We **hiked** through the forest last Saturday.
Lucas **went** sightseeing in Cairo yesterday.
When he was a student, James **rode** a motorcycle to school.

2. 過去の状態

After college, Ryan **became** an IT manager.
At that time, Pamela **lived** in Italy.

3. 過去の事実

George Washington **was** the first President of the United States.

Unit 2
Why Does a Week Have Seven Days?

▶ progressive forms / future tense

なぜ1週間は7日なのでしょうか。不思議に思ったことはありませんか。世界では1週間が5日や6日の国もあります。キリスト教では天地創造（神は6日間で天地を創造し、7日目に休息したこと）から、1週間を7日としています。

Warm-up Questions

次の質問に英語で答えなさい。

1. What do you usually do in your free time?
2. What are you planning to do this weekend?

1 Vocabulary

英文の空所に入れる最も適切な単語を語群より選び、(A) ～ (G) で答えなさい。

(A) attempt	(B) century	(C) cultural	(D) experiments
(E) islands	(F) represents	(G) traditional	

1. The Statue of Liberty in New York City _____ freedom for people everywhere.

2. Bowing instead of shaking hands is one _____ difference between Japan and most other countries.

3. In high school, my favorite subject was science because I liked doing _____.

4. Hawaii is made of eight major _____ and lots of smaller ones.

5. The American inventor Thomas Alva Edison tried many times to make a light bulb before his final _____ succeeded.

6. It makes me sad that _____ Japanese customs like wearing kimonos are slowly disappearing.

7. In English, ten years is called a decade, and one hundred years is known as a _____.

2 Reading 05

For centuries, countries all over the world have been using the seven-day week. But some countries do not have seven days in the week. Java, an island in Indonesia, uses a week with five days. This five-day week is used for cultural and traditional events.

In Nigeria, some people use the Igbo calendar, which has a four-day week. Each day represents one of the four directions, North, South, East, and West. Some Nigerians even name their children after the day of the week they were born on!

Some other countries have tried to use a different number of days in a week. The most interesting attempt was in Russia in the 1930s. In order to increase worker productivity, Russia tried to create new weeks that had either five or six days. The days were renamed after different colors and numbers. This experiment didn't work, however, and Russia soon returned to the seven-day week.

Notes **Java**「ジャワ島」 **Nigeria**「ナイジェリア」 **the Igbo calendar**「イボ暦」 **rename after**「～にちなんで名前を変える」

Reading Comprehension

A True or False

次の英文が本文の内容と一致する場合は T、一致しない場合は F を選びなさい。

1. Countries all over the world have used a seven-day week for a long time. **[T F]**

2. The island of Java uses a week that has only four days. **[T F]**

3. In Nigeria, some people have names that tell what day of the week they were born on. **[T F]**

B Skimming and Scanning

本文の内容について、最も適切な答えを (A) ～ (C) から選びなさい。

1. In what country is the island of Java located?
(A) Indonesia (B) Nigeria (C) Russia

2. What kind of calendar do some people in Nigeria use?
(A) the direction calendar (B) the Igbo calendar (C) the Russian calendar

3. In what decade did Russia try to create weeks with different numbers of days?
(A) The 1900s (B) The 1930s (C) The 1950s

3 Conversation

A Listen and Write

06

次の会話を聞いて、（　　）に単語を書きなさい。

M: What are your plans for the upcoming long weekend?
W: I'm going camping with my family. How [1](　　　　　　　) you?
M: I'm not sure. Maybe I'll just stay here in the city.
W: That's not a bad [2](　　　　　　　). Maybe you'll discover a new place to hang out.
M: Actually, I was thinking about doing something a bit [3](　　　　　　　) energetic.
W: Like what?
M: Like [4](　　　　　　　) in my pajamas all weekend and playing video games.

Notes **hang out**「出かける」 **energetic**「活動的な」 **Like what?**「例えば、どのような」

B Listen and Choose

07

質問を聞いて、（　　）に単語を書き、最も適切な答えを (A) ～ (C) から選びなさい。

1. What will the woman (　　　) (　　　　　　　) the (　　　　) weekend?
(A) Discover a new place
(B) Go camping with her family
(C) Stay home and relax

2. Why will the man be allowed to (　　　　) (　　　　　　　) (　　　　) weekend?
(A) Because he will do something exciting
(B) Because he will go out into the city to look for a new place
(C) Because he will play video games at home

4 Text Completion

次の文章を読んで、空所に入れる最も適切なものを (A) ～ (C) から選びなさい。

Nowadays, the weekend is a time to relax and take a break from __1__ or studying. Most people dream all week about all the stuff that they are __2__ to do on Saturday and Sunday. But people didn't always have two-day weekends. In fact, it was more common for workers to work for six days and to have only one day off. It wasn't until the middle of the 1800s that __3__.

1. (A) works　(B) worked　(C) working
2. (A) go　(B) going　(C) gone
3. (A) a week had seven days
(B) people worked seven days a week
(C) workers had two days off

5 Grammar Check

A (　　) 内の最も適切な語句を選び、英文を完成しなさい。

1. My sister and her friend Mike (am jogging / are jogging / were jogging) now.
2. My brother (are writing / is writing / was writing) in his diary when I saw him in the library.
3. At the moment, Kate (is staying / was staying / will be staying) at her grandmother's house.
4. Last night, at seven, Lily (is cooking / was cooking / will be cooking) dinner.
5. When (Miki is starting / is Miki starting / Miki starts) university?
6. When Zach arrived, we (are playing / were playing / will be playing) cards.
7. This time tomorrow, we (have been celebrating / were celebrating / will be celebrating) Tom's birthday.

B 空所に入れる最も適切な単語を語群から選び、現在進行形か過去進行形の英文にしなさい。

drive	get	have	jump	sit	take

1. "Where is my grandma?" "She __________ on a chair outside in the sunshine."
2. The telephone rang while Rashad __________ a bath.
3. We have to go now. It __________ late.
4. The swimmers __________ into the pool right now.
5. I saw a beautiful sunset while I __________ along the highway.
6. We __________ a barbecue tomorrow. Would you like to come?

C 空所に入れる最も適切な単語を語群より選び、will か現在進行形 (be＋-ing) を使って英文を完成しなさい。

clear	come	do	drink	fly	~~have~~	turn

e.g. "Are you ready to order?" "Yes. I **will have** the fried chicken."

1. A new Marvel movie __________ out next week.
2. Thank you for your advice. I __________ my best!
3. It is so hot in this room! I __________ on the air conditioner.
4. "Would you like tea or coffee?" "I __________ coffee."
5. I am not certain, but I think the weather __________ up this afternoon.
6. Sally has bought an airline ticket online. She __________ to Los Angeles tomorrow.

6 Composition

A 日本語を参考にして、(　　) 内の単語を正しく並べ替え、また [　　] ア～ウに単語を書いて、文章を完成しなさい。

Do you remember ア[　　　　　　] the days-of-the-week song in English in イ[　　　　　　] school? For me, it was a [1](and remember / fun / practice / to / way) the names of the days of the week. In fact, many languages [2](around / have / own / the world / their) songs for remembering the days of the week. Many of these [3](include / with / seven days / songs / starting) Sunday or Monday. But do you know why a week ウ[　　　　] seven days?

小学校で1週間の曜日の歌を英語で歌ったことを覚えていますか。私にとって、それは曜日の名前を練習して覚える楽しい方法でした。実際、世界中の多くの言語には独自の曜日を覚える歌があります。これらの歌の多くは、日曜日か月曜日から始まる7つの日を含みます。しかし、なぜ1週間に7日あるのか知っていますか。

Word Order:

1.

2.

3.

B 次の質問に、(　　) 内の語句を使って答えなさい。

1. What are your plans for the upcoming weekend?
(If I have time / I will go)

2. Do you think there should be more school days in a week? Why?
(If we had one more day / we wouldn't have so much more)

Grammar Spotlight

▶進行形

1. 現在進行形 < be 動詞の現在形 + -ing >

「今～している」と動作が現在進行中であることを表します。

Bruce **is playing** a video game now.

現在進行形の否定文は be 動詞の後ろに not を置きます。

The child **is not playing** in the park today.

疑問文は be 動詞を主語の前に置きます。

Are you writing your report?

2. 過去進行形 < be 動詞の過去形 + -ing >

「～していた」と過去のある時点で動作が進行中であったことを表します。

When I called her, she **was having** dinner.

3. 未来進行形 < will be + -ing >

「～している」と動作が未来のある時点で進行中であることを表します。

They **will be playing** soccer at this time tomorrow.

4. 現在完了進行形 < have / has + been + -ing >

「ずっと～している」と動作が過去のある時点から現在まで続いてきたことを表します。

It **has been raining** for a week.（継続）

☞ 現在完了（have / has +過去分詞）よりも継続の意味が強い。

5. 過去完了進行形 < had + been + -ing >

「ずっと～していた」と動作が過去のある時点まで続いていたことを表します。

Brian was tired because he **had been jogging**.

▶未来形

It **will** be hot next week.　　＜単純未来＞（意志を含まない）

I **will** study hard to become an IT engineer.

＜意志未来＞（話し手の意志を表す）

☞ be + -ing, be going to, be about to も未来を表します。

▶will と現在進行形 (be + -ing) の違い

will: 未来の予想、主語の意志

I **will** be 20 next Friday.　　（意志を含まない未来、予想）

I'm tired. I **will** take a rest.　　（主語の意志）

現在進行形 (be + -ing): 近い未来、前から決めていた確実な予定

It's already 10 p.m. I'**m leaving** now.　　（近い未来）

We **are having** a meeting on Wednesday morning.　　（確実な予定）

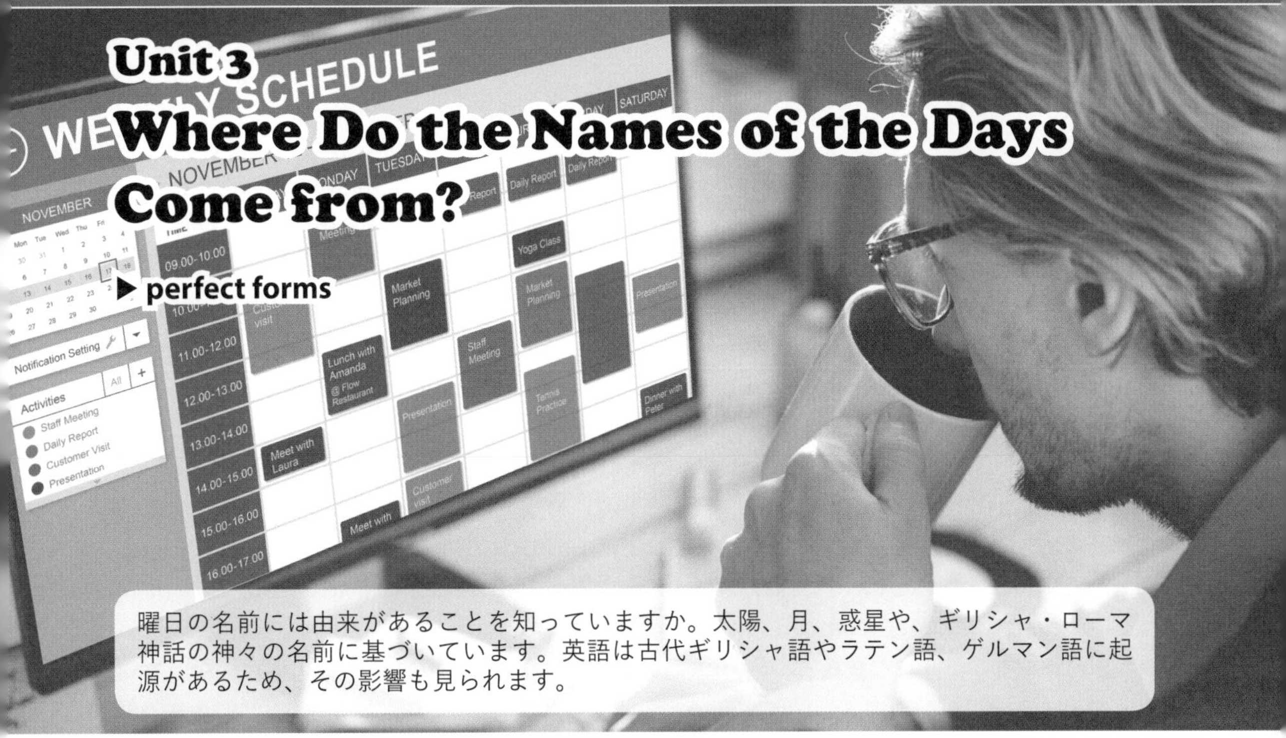

Unit 3
Where Do the Names of the Days Come from?

▶ **perfect forms**

曜日の名前には由来があることを知っていますか。太陽、月、惑星や、ギリシャ・ローマ神話の神々の名前に基づいています。英語は古代ギリシャ語やラテン語、ゲルマン語に起源があるため、その影響も見られます。

Warm-up Questions

次の質問に英語で答えなさい。

1. What is your least favorite day of the week? Why?
2. In English, what day of the week is the most difficult for you to pronounce?

1 Vocabulary

英文の空所に入れる最も適切な単語を語群より選び、(A) ~ (G) で答えなさい。

(A) agriculture	(B) ancient	(C) culture	(D) important
(E) originated	(F) replaced	(G) thunder	

1. Language, festivals, art, food, and clothing are all part of people's _____.
2. I really don't like storms, especially when they have _____ and lightning.
3. Some common Japanese foods like ramen and tempura actually _____ in other countries.
4. These days, many people who study _____ learn how to grow organic vegetables and fruit.
5. It is _____ for us to learn English because English is used all over the world in business, government, and leisure.
6. Legends are _____ stories about heroes and historical figures from a long time ago.
7. Today, digital music has almost _____ music recorded on CDs.

2 Reading

08

Some of the names of days of the week originated in Ancient Rome, where Latin was the main spoken and written language. The Sun (in Latin *sol*) and the Moon (*luna*) were very important to the ancient Romans, so each had its own day: "the Day of the Sun", *dies solis*, and "the Day of the Moon", *dies lunae*.

The ancient Romans had also worshipped many gods, and some of these gods had their own day, too. The god of war, Mars, for example, had *dies Martis*. The messenger of the gods, Mercury, had *dies Mercurii*. Jupiter, the god of thunder, had *dies Jovis*. Venus, the goddess of love, had *dies Veneris*. And Saturn, the god of agriculture, had *dies Saturni*.

Today, Romance languages like Spanish and Italian still use these Roman/Latin names for the days of the week. But English is a little different. Much of the English language comes from an old German language called Anglo-Saxon. Anglo-Saxon speakers replaced many Roman/Latin words—including some of the names of the days of the week—with words from Norse culture. (See **Text Completion** on the next page for how the English names for the days of the week came about.)

Notes　***dies solis***「ディエス ソリス」太陽神、太陽の日　***dies lunae***「ディエス ルナエ」月の女神、月の日　***dies Martis***「ディエス マリティス」軍神、火星の日　***dies Mercurii***「ディエス メルクリ」知恵の神、水星の日　***dies Jovis***「ディエス ヨヴィス」雷の神、木星の日　***dies Veneris***「ディエス ウェネリス」愛の女神、金星の日　***dies Saturni***「ディエス サトゥルニ」農耕神、土星の日　**Norse**「古代スカンジナビア」

Reading Comprehension

A True or False

次の英文が本文の内容と一致する場合は T、一致しない場合は F を選びなさい。

1. Some of the names of the days of the week came from the names of old Roman gods. **[T F]**

2. Jupiter was the only Roman god who didn't have a day named after him. **[T F]**

3. Nowadays, no countries use the old Roman/Latin names for the days of the week. **[T F]**

B Skimming and Scanning

本文の内容について、空所に入れる最も適切なものを (A) ～ (C) から選びなさい。

1. Mars was the Roman god of _____.
(A) love　(B) money　(C) war

2. Saturn was the Roman god of _____.
(A) agriculture　(B) fertility　(C) messages

3. English replaced many Latin words—including some of the names of the days of the week—with words from _____ culture.
(A) Italian　(B) Norse　(C) Spanish

3 Conversation

A Listen and Write

09

次の会話を聞いて、(　　) に単語を書きなさい。

M: Hey, what happened? Where were you last Thursday?
W: I'm sorry? What do you mean?
M: We made [1](　　　　　　) to meet for lunch, but you didn't show up!
W: Was that last [2](　　　　　　)? I thought we were supposed to [3](　　　　　　) this Thursday.
M: Really?
W: Yes. I am so sorry. I have been very busy [4](　　　　　　), and sometimes I get confused. Let me make it up to you. Let's have lunch now. It's on me.

Notes　**show up**「姿を見せる」　**make it up**「埋め合わせをする」　**it's on me**「おごるよ」

B Listen and Choose

10

質問を聞いて、(　　) に単語を書き、最も適切な応答を (A) ～ (C) から選びなさい。

1. (　　　　) (　　　) the man (　　　　　)?
(A) Because he and the woman had made plans to meet, but she didn't show up
(B) Because the woman is always too busy to have lunch with him
(C) Because the woman was late for their planned lunch

2. (　　　　) (　　　　) the woman think they (　　　　) (　　　　　)?
(A) Last Thursday　　(B) This Thursday　　(C) Today, for lunch

4 Text Completion

次の文章を読んで、空所に入れる最も適切なものを (A) ～ (C) から選びなさい。

The English name for Saturday still comes from the Roman/Latin *dies Saturni*, but the Anglo-Saxons ____1____ the names of many other days. The Roman/Latin names *sol* and *luna* ____2____ with the German words *Sunnan* and *Mond*, and became Sunday and Monday. The Norse god of war, Tiu, replaced Mars and became the English name Tuesday. Woden replaced Mercury to become Wednesday; Thor, the god of thunder, replaced Jupiter, and gave us Thursday. And Freya, the goddess of love and fertility, ____3____.

1. (A) changed　　(B) has changed　　(C) was changed

2. (A) replaced　　(B) has replaced　　(C) were replaced

3. (A) replaced Venus to become English's Friday
(B) have replaced Venus instead of Friday
(C) was replaced by Venus to be renamed Friday

5 Grammar Check

A (　　) 内の適切な語句を選び、英文を完成しなさい。

1. I (went / have been) to New Zealand several times since 2015.
2. Judy (worked / has worked) in the restaurant all day yesterday.
3. Sam (arrived / have arrived) in San Francisco two days ago.
4. I (knew / have known) Marc's family since I was a child.
5. The last time I (went / have gone) to the U.K., I visited Wales and Ireland.
6. Kathy and Lee (wanted / have wanted) to go to Spain for a long time.

B (　　) 内の適切な語句を選び、現在完了形の英文にしなさい。

1. A: I (have already seen / have seen already) this movie.
   B: Really? I (have seen / have not seen) it yet. Is it any good?
2. A: (Have you finished / Had you finished) writing the report yet?
   B: I (have finished just / have just finished) it. Here it is.
3. Don (has not spoken / already has spoken) to his teacher yet. I think he will talk to her this afternoon.
4. Please keep what I told you a secret. I (have never told / have told) anyone else yet.

C 空所に入れる動詞を語群より選び、現在完了形にして英文を完成しなさい。

grow	improve	paint	pay	play

1. My English ____________________ a lot since I started studying in England.
2. Don't sit on the bench. I ____________________ it, and it is still wet. (just を使って)
3. James ____________________ the bill and has left a tip for the server.
4. The grass in the park ____________________ very long over the past few months.
5. I ____________________ soccer for five years, so I'm a pretty good player now.

6 Composition

A 日本語を参考にして、(　　) 内の単語を正しく並べ替え、また [　　] ア～ウに単語を書いて、文章を完成しなさい。

In Portuguese, the days of [1](are / easy / remember / the week / to). Sunday [2](after / for / is / named / the word) God, *Domingo*. Monday is the second day, *Segundo-feira*, which ア[　　　　　] "second fair." *Terça-feira* or "third fair" is Tuesday; and *Quarta-feira* or "fourth fair" is Wednesday. *Quinta-feira* or イ"[　　　　　] fair" is Thursday, and Friday is *Sexta-feira*. The [3](comes / day / last / of / the week) from "Shabbat," the day of ウ[　　　　　], and is called *Sabado*.

ポルトガル語では、週の曜日は覚えやすいです。日曜日は「ドミンゴ」という神を表す単語にちなんで名付けられています。月曜日は２日目で、２番目の日を意味する「セグンダフェイラ」です。３番目の日「テルサフェイラ」は火曜日で、４番目の日「クアルタフェイラ」は水曜日です。５番目の日「キンタフェイラ」は木曜日で、金曜日は「セスタフェイラ」です。週の最後の日は休みの日である「シャバット」に由来し、「サバド（安息日）」と呼ばれます。

Word Order:

1. ....

2. ....

3. ....

B 次の質問に、(　　)内の語句を使って答えなさい。

1. Have you eaten lunch already?

(have not eaten / hungry)

....

....

....

....

....

2. What homework did you have to do last weekend? Did you finish it?

(I had to finish / I have not finished)

....

....

....

....

....

Grammar Spotlight

▶完了形

1. 現在完了形 < have / has ＋過去分詞>

現在までの完了・結果、経験、継続 を表します。

Ava **has** just **cleaned** her room.

＜完了・結果＞「(ちょうど) ～したところだ」「(もう) ～した」

I **have been** to Paris before.

＜経験＞「～したことがある」

The weather **has been** fine since last Sunday.

＜継続＞「(ずっと) ～している」

(1) 現在完了形の否定文、疑問文の語順

I **haven't met** Steve yet.　＜主語＋ **have / has** ＋ **not** ＋ 過去分詞＞
Have you **met** Steve?　＜ **have / has** ＋主語 ＋ 過去分詞＞

(2) 現在完了形とよく共に使う語

完了：already, just, yet
経験：before, ever, once, never
継続：for, since

Inez **has never met** my aunt.　「一度も～ない」
The bus **hasn't arrived yet**.　「まだ (～ない)」
Have you **eaten** breakfast **yet**?　「もう (～した)」

☞ yet は否定文と疑問文で使用し、文の終わりに置きます。

(3) 現在完了形は、現在とつながりのない過去を表す副詞 (ago, just now, last week [month, year], yesterday) や when と共に使用できません。

× I **have been** to Italy twice when I was young.
○ I **went** to Italy twice when I was young.

2. 過去完了形 < had ＋ 過去分詞 >

過去のある時点までの完了・結果、経験、継続を表します。

When Alec arrived at the stop, the bus **had** already **left**.

＜完了・結果＞「(すでに) ～してしまっていた」

3. 未来完了形 < will ＋ have ＋ 過去分詞 >

未来のある時点における完了・結果、経験、継続を表します。

I **will have finished** my paper by tomorrow afternoon.

＜完了・結果＞「～しているだろう」

Unit 4
A "Rain Check" in Baseball

▶passive forms

野球で使われる単語やフレーズは日常会話でもよく使用されます。例えば "rain check" は「またの機会」という意味ですが、もともと試合が雨で中止になることに由来します。野球用語から生まれた表現について考えてみましょう。

Warm-up Questions

次の質問に英語で答えなさい。

1. What sports do you like to play or watch?

2. How many professional baseball games have you ever been to?

1 Vocabulary

英文の空所に入れる最も適切な単語を語群より選び、(A) ～ (G) で答えなさい。

(A) another	(B) appointment	(C) attend	(D) cancelled
(E) national	(F) pastime	(G) popular	

1. Many Japanese manga such as *One Piece* and *Dragonball* are very _____ around the globe.

2. One way to learn English is to watch movies in English; _____ way is to read English books.

3. I'm really excited because I'm going to _____ a live concert at Tokyo Dome on Saturday night.

4. Playing video games is the number one _____ among teenagers today.

5. The eagle and the rose are the _____ bird and flower of the U.S., respectively.

6. When you make plans to meet someone, you should arrive fifteen minutes before your _____ time.

7. All of our classes were _____ this week because of the earthquake.

2 Reading

11

Baseball is called "America's national pastime." The modern game of baseball was invented in New York in the mid-1800s. Since then, baseball has become an important part of American culture and history.

Today, baseball is played all over the world, especially in countries like Japan, Australia, Taiwan, Korea, and the Netherlands. In fact, baseball has become one of the world's most popular sports. Over 35 million people from 77 countries play baseball—and countless millions of fans follow it faithfully.

Because of the game's popularity, many words and expressions from baseball are used in everyday English. For example, when people cannot make an appointment, or accept an invitation, they often say "May I have a rain check?" When a baseball game is "rained out"—cancelled because of rain—fans are given a make-up ticket, known as a "rain check." They can use this ticket to attend another game later on. So, in everyday conversation, when we say, "May I have a rain check?" we are asking if we can meet up at another time.

Notes **national pastime**「国民的娯楽」 **millions of**「何百人もの」 **be "rained out"**「雨で中止になる」 **rain check**「雨天順延券」 **make-up**「埋め合わせ（のための）」

Reading Comprehension

A True or False

次の英文が本文の内容と一致する場合は T、一致しない場合は F を選びなさい。

1. Baseball was invented in the mid-1900s. [T F]
2. Baseball is no longer one of the most popular sports around the globe. [T F]
3. When a baseball game is "rained out," fans can receive a ticket to watch a make-up game later on. [T F]

B Skimming and Scanning

本文の内容について、最も適切な答えを (A) ～ (C) から選びなさい。

1. In what city did modern baseball originate?
   (A) Los Angeles (B) New York (C) Tokyo
2. How many people play baseball around the world?
   (A) 350,000 (B) 3,500,000 (C) 35,000,000
3. If you cannot attend an event or make an appointment for some reason but want to go at another time, what can you say?
   (A) "Do you have a rain ticket?"
   (B) "May I have a rain check?"
   (C) "Will you check the rain?"

3 Conversation

A Listen and Write

12

次の会話を聞いて、(　　) に単語を書きなさい。

W: How did your date go?
M: I think I struck out with her.
W: Oh no! What happened?
M: Well, first we [1](　　　　　　) a baseball game.
W: That sounds like [2](　　　　　　)!
M: Yeah, it was. But then, I [3](　　　　　　) to surprise her after the game, so I took her to a fancy seafood restaurant.
W: What's [4](　　　　　　) with that?
M: She is allergic to seafood.

Notes **strike out**「失敗する」 **sound like**「～のようだ」 **fancy**「高級な」

B Listen and Choose

13

質問を聞いて、(　　) に単語を書き、最も適切な応答を (A) ～ (C) から選びなさい。

1. (　　　　) (　　　　) the man's date?
(A) It was okay. (B) It was very good. (C) It was very bad.

2. (　　　　) (　　　　) did the man (　　　　) (　　　　) (　　　　) date?
(A) He took the woman to a baseball game, but she doesn't like baseball.
(B) He took the woman to a seafood restaurant, but she couldn't eat seafood.
(C) He wanted to see the woman again, but she asked for a rain check.

4 Text Completion

次の文章を読んで、空所に入れる最も適切なものを (A) ～ (C) から選びなさい。

Another baseball expression that comes from baseball is *hit or miss*. Perhaps you have heard someone say something __1__, "I don't know if the movie will be any good or not. These kinds of movies are *hit or miss*." In baseball, when a batter __2__ at the ball, he will either hit it or miss it. So, when we say that something is *hit or miss*, it means it might be good or bad. __3__

1. (A) as (B) like (C) that

2. (A) swings (B) swung (C) swinging

3. (A) It will not be any good at all.
(B) You can be certain it will be great.
(C) We can't know for sure until we see it.

5 Grammar Check

A (　　) 内の最も適切な語句を選び、英文を完成しなさい。

1. The player's big contract (signed / will be signed / was signed) tomorrow.
2. Sally (isn't invited / invite / are invited) to the party.
3. The beautiful luxury car (was made in / has made at / had made to) Germany.
4. The kindergarten children (saw / have seen / were seen) crossing the street with their teacher.
5. Cathy (catches to / is caught by / was caught in) a heavy downpour last night.
6. Sam (may allow in / are allowed / was allowed) to take a make-up test a few days later.
7. The large oil painting entitled "Guernica" (created / was created / will be created) by Picasso in 1937.
8. Your package (delivers / is being delivered / is delivering) by either UPS or Nippon Express.

B 2 つの英文 (a) (b) が同じ内容になるように、見出しの動詞を適切な形にして英文を完成しなさい。

1. (read)
   (a) Dad ________________ the newspaper every morning.
   (b) The newspaper ________________ Dad every morning.
2. (make)
   (a) Sharon is ________________ all our travel plans.
   (b) All our travel plans ________________ by Sharon.
3. (give)
   (a) The manager will ________________ you instructions.
   (b) Instructions will ________________ you by the manager.
4. (please)
   (a) The result of the exam that Peter took the other day ________________ him.
   (b) Peter ________________ the result of the exam that he took the other day.

C 次の能動態を受動態に書き換えなさい。

1. Did Nick write the article?
   ....
2. Alice will speak the truth.
   ....
3. Are they singing a rap song?
   ....
4. I won't send the document until tomorrow.
   ....
5. Snow covered the village at dawn.
   ....

6 Composition

A 日本語を参考にして、(　　) 内の単語を正しく並べ替え、また [　　] ア～ウに単語を書いて、文章を完成しなさい。

Baseball is a [ア] [　　　　　] sport. People [1](countries / in / know / many / the meaning) of the expression “home run.” In fact, [イ] [　　　　　] “home run” is used in different everyday situations [ウ] [　　　　　] as business or education, anyone anywhere will understand that [2](doing / it / means / well / something). Everyday English [3](a lot / baseball / expressions / of / uses) like “home run.” How many do you know?

野球は人気のあるスポーツです。たくさんの国の人々が、「ホームラン」という表現の意味を知っています。実際、「ホームラン」がビジネスや教育のような様々な日常の状況で使用されるとき、どこの誰でもそれが何かをうまくやっていることを意味するのがわかるでしょう。日常英語は「ホームラン」のような野球由来の表現をたくさん使用します。あなたはどれぐらい多く知っていますか。

Word Order:

1. ....

2. ....

3. ....

B 次の質問に、(　　) 内の語句を使って答えなさい。

1. Do you follow professional or high school baseball? Why or why not?
(I enjoy watching / I actually prefer to)

2. Walt Disney once said, “If you can dream it, you can do it.” Do you have any favorite quotes?
(one of my favorite quotes is / it reminds me)

Grammar Spotlight

▶受動態

受動態は、主語が動作を受ける対象になる文で、「(主語が) ～される」という受け身の形で使われます。

1. 受動態：be 動詞＋過去分詞＋(by ～)

The bathroom **is cleaned** by me every day.
The products **are tested** by factory workers.
The novel **was written** by an Egyptian author.

2. 能動態と受動態の書き換え

未来形の受動態 ＜will + be + 過去分詞＞

I **will meet** my friends in the library.
→ My friends **will be met** by me in the library.

進行形の受動態 ＜be + being + 過去分詞＞

Kitty **is eating** pizza.
→ Pizza **is being eaten** by Kitty.

完了形の受動態 ＜have / has + been + 過去分詞＞

I **have finished** the report.
→ The report **has been finished** by me.

3. by 以外の前置詞を使う受動態

The singer **is known to** everyone.
I **was surprised at** the news.
The house **is built of** wood.
The mountain **was covered with** snow.

Unit 5
A "Fumble" in Football

▶ infinitives / gerunds

アメリカンフットボールは、アメリカで最も人気のあるスポーツの１つです。日常用いる言葉に、フットボールに由来するものがあります。ボールを落とすことをファンブルと言いますが、日常会話ではどのような意味で使っているでしょうか。

Warm-up Questions

次の質問に英語で答えなさい。

1. How much do you know about American football and its rules?
2. What do you think of "contact sports" like football or boxing?

1 Vocabulary

英文の空所に入れる最も適切な単語を語群より選び、(A) ～ (G) で答えなさい。

(A) achieve	(B) business	(C) goal	(D) mistakes
(E) nervous	(F) responsibility	(G) simple	

1. I don't like to make presentations because I feel really _____ when I talk in front of people.
2. Teachers have a _____ to help their students learn and do well.
3. This year, I want to lose five kilograms. What is your _____ for this year?
4. "Hi!" is a short, _____ and friendly way to say "Hello."
5. This year, I want to get 900 on the TOEIC. What should I do to _____ that?
6. Henry is majoring in _____ and management because he hopes to become an entrepreneur one day.
7. Although most of us hate to make _____, errors can be a good thing if we learn from them.

2 Reading

Although it might seem complicated, American football is actually a simple game. One team—known as the offense—must get the ball across the field to the other end or goal. The other team—the defense—tries to stop them. The offense can move the ball by running with it, or by throwing (passing) it from one teammate to another. Play stops when the ball or the person running with the ball touches the ground.

Football is a team sport. Every person on the field has a certain responsibility to help the team win. If everyone does what they are supposed to, the team will achieve its goal. Because of football's focus on working together, some football words and expressions are used in business. As in football, people who work in business have different responsibilities and must cooperate to succeed.

Every so often, we all make mistakes. In football, one common mistake comes when a player drops the ball. This is called a fumble. That's why when you make a mistake in business, you can say something like, "I was so nervous that I fumbled my presentation."

Notes　**every so often**「時々」　**fumble**「(名) ファンブル、(動) ファンブルする」ボールを落とすこと、落とす　**that's why**「だから～なのだ」

Reading Comprehension

A True or False

次の英文が本文の内容と一致する場合は T、一致しない場合は F を選びなさい。

1. American football is a very complicated and difficult sport to understand. **[T F]**

2. The goal of American football is to move the ball across the field to your opponent's goal. **[T F]**

3. In American football, play stops when the ball touches the ground. **[T F]**

B Skimming and Scanning

本文の内容について、最も適切な答えを (A) ～ (C) から選びなさい。

1. In American football, what is one way that a team can move the ball?
(A) By kicking it　(B) By rolling it　(C) By throwing it

2. What kind of sport does the writer say American football is?
(A) A dangerous sport　(B) A team sport　(C) A children's game

3. What does it mean when someone "fumbles" something?
(A) The person does something well.
(B) The person make a mistake.
(C) The person works in business.

3 Conversation

A Listen and Write

15

次の会話を聞いて、(　　) に単語を書きなさい。

W: Did you see the game between the Cowboys and the Dolphins last night?

M: I sure did! It was so [1](　　　　　　　). It came down to the last minute.

W: I thought it was over when one of the Cowboys [2](　　　　　　　) on the 15-yard line.

M: Me, too. But luckily, the Cowboys were able to get the ball [3](　　　　　　　) and score on the next play.

W: All in all, the Cowboys played very well. They [4](　　　　　　　) to be this year's Super Bowl champions.

Notes　**come down to the last minute**「土壇場に来る」　**be over**「終わる」　**all in all**「全体として」
Super Bowl champion「スーパーボール・チャンピオン」アメリカンフットボール優勝チーム

B Listen and Choose

16

質問を聞いて、(　　) に単語を書き、最も適切な応答を (A) ～ (C) から選びなさい。

1. (　　　　　) (　　　　　) the game so (　　　　　　　　　) (　　　　) (　　　　　)?

(A) It wasn't decided until the very end.

(B) There were so many fumbles.

(C) There were so many fans at the game.

2. (　　　　) (　　　　) last (　　　　　　　) (　　　　　)?

(A) The Cowboys did.　(B) The Dolphins did.　(C) Neither team did. It was a tie.

4 Text Completion

次の文章を読んで、空所に入れる最も適切なものを (A) ～ (C) から選びなさい。

In football, when it seems as if a team is about to lose, they will make one last try at __1__ the game. Usually, this does not work, but it is important never __2__ up! This last try is called a "Hail Mary." So, the next time you think __3__, don't give up! Try a Hail Mary!

1. (A) win　(B) winning　(C) to win

2. (A) gives　(B) giving　(C) to give

3. (A) you will not succeed

(B) you will play football

(C) you will win the game

Notes　**Hail Mary**「ヘイルメアリー」ロングパス

5 Grammar Check

A (　　) 内の適切な語句を選び、英文を完成しなさい。

1. Marie was asked (to participate / participating) in the new project.
2. I can touch my toes without (to bend / bending) my knees.
3. We invited our high school classmates (to attend / attending) our wedding reception.
4. Peter was fined for (to drive / driving) twenty miles an hour over the speed limit.
5. Would you please ask Mr. Edwards (to check / checking) his email?
6. I'll ask my secretary (to give / giving) him the report by the end of the day.

B (　　) 内の最も適切なものを選び、英文を完成しなさい。

1. Grace likes (to cook / cooking / どちらも可) when she has time.
2. Tracy advised me (to take / taking / どちらも可) that new accounting course.
3. I really enjoy (to hike / hiking / どちらも可) in the forest on crisp fall days.
4. Beth began (to sing / singing / どちらも可) pop songs when she was only three years old.
5. Joshua has to finish (to write / writing / どちらも可) his application essay by April 15.

C 空所に入れる語を語群より選び、不定詞か動名詞にして英文を完成しなさい。

look	shut	study	wash	work

1. Derek spends every morning ________________ English. He is a diligent student.
2. I am getting tired of ________________ at the same job every day.
3. Please remember ________________ down your computer before you leave the office.
4. I think it is time ________________ your car. It is so dirty.
5. After weeks of searching, the police eventually stopped ________________ for the criminal.

6 Composition

A 日本語を参考にして、(　　) 内の単語を正しく並べ替え、また [　　] ア～ウに単語を書いて、文章を完成しなさい。

American football is not very popular in most parts of the world. Other sports [ア][　　　　　] soccer, basketball, and rugby have a lot more fans abroad. However, in the U.S., football is [イ][　　　　　] very popular. Each year, more [1](children / football / play / than / two million) for their community or school team, more than [2](attend / college / football / people / 40 million) games, and over [ウ][　　　　　] million people watch [3](biggest / in / game / professional football / the), the Super Bowl, on TV.

アメリカンフットボールは世界のほとんどの場所で、あまり人気がありません。外国では、サッカーやバスケットボール、ラグビーのような他のスポーツに、ずっと多くのファンがいます。しかしアメリカでは、フットボールは、やはり非常に人気があります。毎年、2百万人以上の子どもたちが、コミュニティーや学校のチームでフットボールをし、4千万人以上が大学のフットボールの試合に参加し、1億1千万人以上がプロフットボールの最大の試合であるスーパーボールをテレビで観戦します。

Word Order:

1. ....

2. ....

3. ....

B 次の質問に、(　　) 内の語句を使って答えなさい。

1. Which do you prefer, working in groups or working by yourself? Why?
(it depends on / I like working)

....

....

....

....

....

2. Do you like watching sports? Why?
(I enjoy watching / because / it is also very exciting to see)

....

....

....

....

....

Grammar Spotlight

▶不定詞

「to + 動詞の原形」を不定詞と言います。
動詞に to を付けることで、名詞や形容詞、副詞の働きをします。

It is Bill's dream **to discover** a new species.「～すること」 ＜名詞的用法＞
Michael has a report **to hand in** today. 「～すべき」 ＜形容詞的用法＞
Laura went to college **to study** science. 「～するために」＜副詞的用法＞

▶動名詞

動詞の原形に -ing を付けた形を動名詞と言います。
名詞の働きをし、主語・補語・目的語・前置詞の目的語になります。

Finding information on the internet is useful. ＜主語＞
My hobby is **playing** the guitar. ＜補語＞
Young people love **using** social media. ＜目的語＞
I'm looking forward to **seeing** him next Monday. ＜前置詞の目的語＞

▶間違いやすい表現

1. 不定詞のみを目的語に取る動詞、動名詞のみを目的語に取る動詞

不定詞：afford, agree, claim, decide, plan, refuse, want, wish, etc.
動名詞：avoid, enjoy, deny, finish, give up, mind, miss, resist, etc.

James **wants to buy** a pair of shoes.
Emily just **finished reading** the novel.

2. 不定詞と動名詞の両方を取り、意味が同じ動詞：like, love, start, begin など

Julia **loves reading [to read]** in her free time.
My mother doesn't **like shopping [to shop]**.

Unit 6
A "Baller" in Basketball

▶modal verbs

NBAと音楽のつながりは深く、試合会場ではヒップホップが流れます。バスケットボールの動きにヒップホップのテンポがよく合います。バスケットボール選手にとって音楽は、試合のモチベーションと集中力を高める手段です。

Warm-up Questions

次の質問に英語で答えなさい。

1. What winter sports do you play or have you played?
2. Do you prefer doing indoor or outdoor activities?

1 Vocabulary

英文の空所に入れる最も適切な単語を語群より選び、(A) ~ (G) で答えなさい。

(A) athletes	(B) describe	(C) increasing	(D) invited
(E) league	(F) professional	(G) released	

1. Many young people dream of becoming _____ players, becoming famous, and making a lot of money.
2. In the U.S., most "pro" sports have their own organization, or what is known as a _____.
3. Before a movie is _____ in theaters, many short video commercials are run on TV that tell us about it.
4. Many professional sports players earn huge salaries. Some people say that these _____ are paid too much.
5. The number of couples who choose not to have children is said to be _____.
6. Famous natural sites like the Grand Canyon and Africa's Victoria Falls are almost too spectacular to _____.
7. In many Western countries, when people are _____ to a special event like a wedding, they will see the abbreviation "R.S.V.P." at the bottom of the invitation, which asks them to respond to the invitation.

2 Reading

17

Basketball may not be the most popular sport in the world (soccer is), but it is the fastest growing among sports fans. In the U.S., the NBA (National Basketball Association), the main professional basketball league, makes almost $5 billion every year. Because of the NBA's success and basketball's increasing renown, you can now find professional basketball leagues in many other countries such as Japan, France, China, and the Philippines.

Surprisingly, in America, hip-hop music and basketball are, in a way, connected. Several famous NBA athletes like Shaquille O'Neal have released hip-hop albums, and some rap artists have even been invited to practice with professional teams. So, it is not surprising to find basketball terminology—words and phrases—used in music and in daily conversation.

One example is the word "baller." Originally, baller meant someone who played basketball exceptionally well. Thanks to the success of NBA stars like Michael Jordan and Kobe Bryant, baller is now often used to describe people who do something well or who are highly successful at what they do. How about you? Are you a baller at anything?

Notes **NBA**「全米バスケットボール協会」 **in a way**「ある意味で」 **rap artist**「ラップアーティスト」 **baller**「ボーラー」バスケットボールの上手な人、成功している人

Reading Comprehension

A True or False

次の英文が本文の内容と一致する場合は T、一致しない場合は F を選びなさい。

1. Basketball has now grown to become the most popular sport in the world. **[T F]**

2. In the U.S., professional basketball and hip-hop are, in a way, related. **[T F]**

3. Originally, "baller" meant an excellent musician. **[T F]**

B Skimming and Scanning

本文の内容について、最も適切な答えや語句を (A) ～ (C) から選びなさい。

1. Which of these is the most popular sport in the world?
(A) Baseball (B) Basketball (C) Soccer

2. In the U.S., the main professional basketball league is called ____.
(A) the Association of American Ballers
(B) the Basketball Association of America
(C) the National Basketball Association

3. Which of these professional basketball players is NOT mentioned in the reading?
(A) Kobe Bryant (B) Lebron James (C) Michael Jordan

3 Conversation

A Listen and Write

18

次の会話を聞いて、(　　) に単語を書きなさい。

M: How did your presentation go?

W: Oh, it was a slam dunk!

M: Good for you! I know how much time and effort you put into [1](　　　　　　　) for it.

W: I really did, and all that preparation and practice really paid off.

M: Well, now that you are all [2](　　　　　　　) with it, what are you going to do next?

W: After all that [3](　　　　　　　) and hard work, I need some exercise. Do you want to go to the [4](　　　　　　　) and shoot some hoops with me?

Notes　**slam dunk**「(バスケットボールの) 強烈なダンクシュート、大成功」**Good for you!**「よかったね！」 **shoot some hoops**「バスケットボールをする」

B Listen and Choose

19

質問を聞いて、(　　) に単語を書き、最も適切な応答を (A) ～ (C) から選びなさい。

1. (　　　　　) (　　　　　) the woman's (　　　　　　　　　　)?

(A) It didn't go well at all.　　(B) It was a big success.　　(C) It was only okay.

2. (　　　　　) (　　　　　) the woman mean when she (　　　　　) (　　　　　) (　　　　　) practicing "paid off"?

(A) That all that practice was very tiring

(B) That her practicing earned her a lot of money

(C) That her practicing helped lead to her success

4 Text Completion

次の文章を読んで、空所に入れる最も適切なものを (A) ～ (C) から選びなさい。

One of __1__ that basketball players make money is through what is known as merchandising. Merchandising is the selling of products like basketball-related clothing and shoes. Because basketball players are __2__ popular, many sporting goods companies such as Nike and Reebok ask players to promote—that is, to help sell—their basketball shoes. But actually, not all of these shoes are used to play basketball. Some shoes like Air Jordans are used __3__.

1. (A) the way　　(B) the ways　　(C) ways

2. (A) extremely　　(B) slightly　　(C) somewhat

3. (A) more as everyday shoes than for playing basketball

(B) more for advertising in television commercials than as shoes for actually playing in

(C) only by hip-hop artists

5 Grammar Check

A (　　) 内の最も適切な語句を選び、英文を完成しなさい。

1. It's quite cold today. Do you think it (ought / supposed to / might) snow later?
2. You (must / shouldn't / won't) leave your door unlocked when you go out. It's dangerous.
3. You have a fever. You (should / shouldn't / shall) see a doctor.
4. My parents say I (can / can't / should) play video games until I've finished my homework.
5. This isn't correct! It (can / must / won't) be a mistake!
6. I am so frustrated! I just (can / can't / shouldn't) understand this question!
7. Applicants for the job must (can / could / be able to) speak English fluently.
8. (May / Must / Will) I go to the washroom, please?

B 空所に can, can't, could, couldn't のいずれかと、語群の適切な動詞を用いて英文を完成しなさい。

find	go	play	lift	take	understand

1. The school cafeteria was full. Jenny ______________________ a seat anywhere.
2. Your father ______________________ a nap on the sofa if he is tired.
3. If it rains tomorrow, I'm afraid we ______________________ on our hike.
4. My sister ______________________ the piano very well when she was young.
5. Greg was speaking so quickly that I ______________________ what he was saying.
6. Beth ______________________ the box. It's too heavy!

C 空所に must have か couldn't have に続くように、語群から動詞を選び、適切な形にして英文を完成しなさい。

arrive	clean	enjoy	put	study

1. Kevin did well on the test. He ______________________ hard.
2. My son's room is still messy. He ______________________ it.
3. Helen looked very happy. She ______________________ last night's movie date.
4. My friends ______________________ on time. A traffic jam held them up.
5. She ______________________ too much sugar in my coffee. It's way too sweet.

6 Composition

A 日本語を参考にして、(　　) 内の単語を正しく並べ替え、また [　　] ア〜ウに単語を書いて、文章を完成しなさい。

Basketball is a relatively new sport. It was invented less ア[　　　　　　] 150 years ago, in a cold gymnasium in Massachusetts. The イ[　　　　　　] of basketball, a Canadian man named James Naismith, [1](a game / make / that / to / wanted) was, as he put it, “interesting, easy to learn, and easy to [2](and / by / in / play / the winter) artificial light.” He created basketball for his ウ[　　　　　　] education class because [3](could / go / his students / not / outside) to play.

バスケットボールは、比較的新しいスポーツです。それはマサチューセッツ州の寒い体育館で考案されてから、まだ150年経っていません。バスケットボールの考案者であるジェームズ・ネイスミスという名のカナダ人は、彼が言っているように、「面白く、覚えやすく、冬に人工光で簡単に遊べる」ゲームを作りたいと思いました。生徒たちが外に行って遊ぶことができなかったので、彼は体育の授業のためにバスケットボールを作ったのです。

Word Order:

1.

2.

3.

B 次の質問に、(　　) 内の語句を使って答えなさい。

1. What kind of shoes do you most often wear?
(I am a fan of / wear casually)

2. How do you choose the shoes you buy?
(For me, comfort is / I want to wear)

Grammar Spotlight

▶助動詞

1.「助動詞＋動詞の原形」で、動詞に意味を加えます。

will：～だろう（未来）、～するつもりだ（意志）　＜過去形は **would**＞
can：～できる（可能）、～してもよい（許可）　＜過去形は **could**＞
may：～してもよい（許可）、～かもしれない（推量）　＜過去形は **might**＞
should：～すべきだ（義務）、～するはずだ（推量）
must：～しなければならない（義務）、～に違いない（推量）

You **can** enjoy seeing tonight's concert online.
I **must** buy a stuffed animal for my daughter.
You **should** fill out the form carefully.
Emily **will** have to go to the beauty salon.
Eric **will** be able to leave the hospital soon.

2. 助動詞＋ have ＋過去分詞

(1) 現在の時点での過去の事柄に対する推量
may have ＋過去分詞「～したかもしれない」
cannot have ＋過去分詞「～したはずがない」
must have ＋過去分詞「～したに違いない」
Stella is late. She **may have taken** the wrong bus.
I can't see Paul. He **must have gone out**.

(2) 過去において行われなかった行為に対する後悔
should have ＋過去分詞「～すべきだったのに（しなかった）」
She failed the test. She **should have studied** harder.

3. 助動詞を含む慣用表現

had better ～「～する方がよい」
may well ～「～するのももっともだ」
cannot help -ing「～せざるをえない」

You **had better** take an umbrella. It's going to rain.
When he said that, I **couldn't help laughing**.

Unit 7
Why Is English Spelling So Difficult?

▶ countable and uncountable nouns / articles

なぜ私たちは英語のスペリングや発音を難しいと感じるのでしょうか。英語はスペリングと発音が必ずしも一致しない場合があり、スペリング通りに読んでも正しく発音するのが難しいのです。さらに発音しない文字もあります。

Warm-up Questions

次の質問に英語で答えなさい。

1. What English words do you have trouble spelling?

2. Do you know how to pronounce these "strange" words?
[aisle debut eighth receipt segue Wednesday]

1 Vocabulary

英文の空所に入れる最も適切な単語を語群より選び、(A) ～ (G) で答えなさい。

(A) borrowed	(B) developing	(C) kept	(D) original
(E) reason	(F) unfortunately	(G) usually	

1. The _____ why I am studying English now is because I want to do a homestay in New Zealand.

2. In English, _____ many words aren't spelled the way they sound, and vice versa.

3. Often, novels and other books are turned into movies. Some people think that the _____ book is better than the movie.

4. Technology is constantly _____ —getting better and easier to use.

5. I _____ listen to music when I study, especially to jazz, because it helps me concentrate.

6. I have _____ all my old comic books since I was in elementary school.

7. Some elderly people in Japan are upset because so many new words these days are _____ from English.

2 Reading

20

Today's English developed from many languages, including Latin, Greek, German, Spanish, and French. Many everyday English words such as *karaoke, ketchup,* or *kindergarten* come from other languages. When English borrows these words, it usually keeps the original spelling. Being able to spell words helps us to understand their pronunciation or sound.

Unfortunately, how a word is pronounced in English is usually different from how it is pronounced in the original language. For example, " カラオケ " in English is spelled as "karaoke," but it is pronounced Ke-ree-OH-kee. This is one reason why English words are so hard to spell.

After the invention of the printing press in the 15th century, English speakers tried to standardize spellings. But back then, the English language was still developing, and people pronounced words differently. For example, in those days, people pronounced the "K" in words like knight and knee, which today have a silent "K."

Notes **printing press**「印刷機」 **back then = in those days**「当時は」

Reading Comprehension

A True or False

次の英文が本文の内容と一致する場合は T、一致しない場合は F を選びなさい。

1. Almost all English words come from one or two other languages. **[T F]**
2. Words from other languages sound the same in English as they do in the original language. **[T F]**
3. In English, the pronunciation of a word and its spelling don't always match. **[T F]**

B Skimming and Scanning

本文の内容について、最も適切な答えを (A) ～ (C) から選びなさい。

1. Which of these English words that come from other languages is NOT mentioned in the reading?
   (A) Banana (B) Karaoke (C) Ketchup
2. When was the printing press invented?
   (A) In the 1100s (B) In the 1400s (C) In the 1700s
3. If you lived in the 15th century, how would you most likely pronounce the word "knee"?
   (A) /knait/ (B) /kni/ (C) /ni/

3 Conversation

A Listen and Write

21

次の会話を聞いて、(　　) に単語を書きなさい。

M: Excuse me. May I ask you a [1](　　　　　　)?
W: Sure. Go ahead.
M: [2](　　　　　　) do you pronounce this word?
W: Let's see. Ah! That's pronounced SKEH-jool.
M: Really? But I [3](　　　　　　) someone say it with a SHEH sound in the first syllable.
W: That's British English. In British English, it is [4](　　　　　　) SHEH-jool.

Notes **go ahead**「どうぞ」 **let's see**「ええと」

B Listen and Choose

22

質問を聞いて、(　　) に単語を書き、最も適切な応答を (A) ～ (C) から選びなさい。

1. (　　　　) (　　　　) the man (　　　　) the woman (　　　　) (　　　　)?
(A) To tell him the meaning of a word
(B) To tell him the spelling of a word
(C) To tell him the pronunciation of a word

2. (　　　　) (　　　　) are the man and woman probably (　　　　) (　　　　)?
(A) schedule　　(B) school　　(C) shelf

4 Text Completion

次の文章を読んで、空所に入れる最も適切なものを (A) ～ (C) から選びなさい。

Samuel Johnson's *Dictionary of the English Language* was published ___1___ 1755. That monumental book marked an important development for the English language. Johnson's *Dictionary* showed the exact spellings and meanings of thousands of words. Johnson's dictionary also included idiomatic and slang words and phrases used by ___2___ in everyday conversations. This helped standardize the English language, and is one reason why English ___3___.

1. (A) at　　(B) by　　(C) in
2. (A) person　　(B) people　　(C) peoples
3. (A) has become a global language
(B) is so difficult to spell
(C) uses words from different languages

Notes ***Dictionary of the English Language***『英語辞典』 **global language**「世界共通語」

5 Grammar Check

A 下線部の名詞が可算名詞ならC (countable)、不可算名詞ならU (uncountable) を選びなさい。

1. The children are studying in the classroom. **(C / U)**
2. I don't like coffee. I prefer tea. **(C / U)**
3. We studied the effects of pollution on the environment. **(C / U)**
4. Would you like butter on your bread? **(C / U)**
5. I must memorize a lot of vocabulary for this test. **(C / U)**
6. Make sure you drink plenty of water when you exercise. **(C / U)**
7. Yesterday, some police officers gave a presentation at my school. **(C / U)**
8. We met some interesting tourists on our vacation. **(C / U)**
9. Oh no! I forgot to put gas in the car! **(C / U)**
10. I have a lot of homework to do this weekend. **(C / U)**

B (　　) に a / an / the / ×（冠詞不要）を入れて、英文を完成しなさい。

1. It's very cold today. I'd better wear (　　) heavy coat.
2. Joanna wants to go to (　　) university after graduating from high school.
3. Michael is training hard to be (　　) engineer.
4. Don't worry. Everyone makes (　　) mistakes sometimes.
5. Carter is (　　) most intelligent person I have ever met.
6. Mom baked (　　) cake yesterday. (　　) cake was delicious.
7. Our meeting begins after (　　) lunch.
8. I arrived here (　　) hour ago.
9. Do you think people will travel to (　　) Mars in the future?
10. Allison earns two thousand dollars (　　) month as a part-time instructor.

C 空所に入れる単語を語群より選び、必要なら適切な形に変えて、英文を完成しなさい。

advice	building	employee	pair	sheet	slice

1. I usually have two ________________ of bread with a cup of coffee for breakfast.
2. David gave me some excellent ________________ before my interview.
3. This town's ________________ are very old, which is why I love them.
4. I bought a ________________ of shoes that were on sale yesterday.
5. Many of the ________________ in this company are very talented.
6. Could you please hand us four ________________ of paper so we can take notes?

6 Composition

A 日本語を参考にして、(　　)内の単語を正しく並べ替え、また[　　]ア～ウに単語を書いて、文章を完成しなさい。

Everyone can ア[　　　　] that learning English is difficult. One of the hardest things about it 1(how / is / learn / to / to spell) English words. There 2(any / be / do not / seem / to) rules to English spelling. This is true 3(are / for / not only / students / who) learning English as a foreign language イ[　　　　] also for ウ[　　　　] speakers. Why is English spelling so weird?

誰もが、英語を学ぶのは難しいということに同意できます。それについて最も難しいことの１つは、英単語の綴り方を学ぶことです。英語のスペリングには何のルールもないように思えます。これは、外国語として英語を学んでいる学生だけでなく、母語話者にも当てはまります。なぜ英語のスペリングはそんなに奇妙なのでしょうか。

Word Order:

1. ....

2. ....

3. ....

B 次の質問に、(　　)内の語句を使って答えなさい。

1. Which is easier for you to understand, British English or American English?
(easier to understand / pronunciations and words)

....

....

....

....

....

2. Do you know any Japanese words that are borrowed from other languages?
(I think / comes from)

....

....

....

....

....

Grammar Spotlight

▶名詞

名詞は人や物、事柄を表し、数えられる名詞と数えられない名詞があります。

1. 数えられる名詞（可算名詞）

普通名詞 (bank, party, train, etc.)

☞ 不定冠詞 (a / an)、定冠詞 (the) が付くか、または複数形になります。

Clark works for a **bank**.
Lisa is going to a **party** this evening.
I often use the **computer** on the **desk**.

集合名詞 (people, family, police, etc.)
My **family** are all very well.
The **police** are investigating the cause of the accident.

2. 数えられない名詞（不可算名詞）

固有名詞 (Germany, Susan, etc.)、物質名詞 (salt, water, etc.)、抽象名詞 (advice, honesty, etc.)

☞ baggage, beer, furniture, health, information, knowledge, news, truth は不可算名詞で、不定冠詞 (a / an) を付けたり複数形にしません。

× She can give you some **informations** about the trip.
○ She can give you some **information** about the trip.

× I have a **good news** for you.
○ I have **good news** for you.

3. 数えられない名詞の数え方

Jacob drank **three glasses** of beer.
・a bottle of wine, a cup of coffee, a sheet of paper, etc.

▶冠詞

1. 不定冠詞 a / an

初めて話題になる数えられる単数名詞の前に付けます。
Stella is **a** student who wears **a** school uniform.
This is **an** interesting new product.

2. 定冠詞 the

可算・不可算、単数・複数を問わず名詞の前に付き、特定のものを表します。
I bought a coat. **The** coat is really warm.（名詞を繰り返すとき）
Please pass me **the** salt.（状況から特定性が明らかな場合）
John uses **the latest** computer.（the ＋形容詞の最上級）

Unit 8
How Do You Make a Hamburger?

▶ **prepositions**

ハンバーガーはアメリカで生まれて以来、子どもから大人まで世界中の人々を幸せにしています。ハンバーガーのバンズに挟むパティは、いろいろな種類がありますが、食肉パティの場合、牛肉だけのパティが最も多いです。

Warm-up Questions

次の質問に英語で答えなさい。

1. Which do you prefer, eating out or eating at home?
2. What is your favorite foreign food?

1 Vocabulary

英文の空所に入れる最も適切な単語を語群より選び、(A) ～ (G) で答えなさい。

(A) boiled	(B) eventually	(C) grill	(D) ingredient
(E) served	(F) shredded	(G) spread	

1. In U.S. restaurants, hamburgers are usually _____ with French fries or onion rings.
2. Why are some _____ eggs so hard to peel and some so easy?
3. Sauerkraut is a kind of pickle that comes from Germany. It is made with _____ cabbage and vinegar.
4. Some people predict that _____, all money will be digital money.
5. I really enjoy going to the beach with friends and cooking meat on a barbecue _____.
6. Did you know that collagen is an _____ in ice cream?
7. A popular sandwich among kids in America is the PBJ, which is peanut butter and jelly or jam _____ on bread.

2 Reading

23

There are all kinds of different ways to make and enjoy a hamburger. You can fry it, grill it, or barbecue it. You can then top it with cheese and a slice of bacon, add lettuce and tomato, and spice it up with mustard, ketchup, and mayonnaise. You can serve it on a hamburger bun or a sliced bagel, or you can put it between two toasted slices of any kind of bread you like. Regardless of how you make, serve, and enjoy your "burger," the one essential ingredient is the all-beef patty.

So why do we call it a hamburger when there's no ham involved? Good question! It is widely believed that the word "hamburger" comes from the name of the city where the dish was supposedly created—Hamburg, Germany. But that "hamburger" was quite different from the hamburger we know today. It was a mixture of shredded or ground beef and various spices that was fried or boiled, and was given the name "Hamburg steak."

Even back then, though, lots of people preferred to eat their Hamburg steak in a bun—like a sandwich. But it still wasn't a "hamburger." That American treat didn't become "all the rage" until it was served at the St. Louis World's Fair in 1904. Soon thereafter, the hamburger as we know it was "selling like hot cakes" at drive-in restaurants all around the United States. Eventually, fast-food chains like McDonald's, Burger King, and Wendy's were serving the whole wide world millions of American "burgers" every single day.

Notes **regardless of**「〜にかかわらず」 **all-beef patty**「オールビーフパティ」牛ミンチ肉を平たく丸くしたもの **Hamburg**「ハンブルグ」ドイツの港町 **shredded**「細切りにした」 **all the rage**「大流行」 **St. Louis World's Fair**「セントルイス万国博覧会」 **sell like hot cakes**「飛ぶように売れる」

Reading Comprehension

A True or False

次の英文が本文の内容と一致する場合は T、一致しない場合は F を選びなさい。

1. There are only one or two ways to make a hamburger. **[T F]**

2. Ham is an important ingredient of any good hamburger. **[T F]**

3. The name "hamburger" comes from a U.S. city where a World's Fair was held. **[T F]**

B Skimming and Scanning

本文の内容について、最も適切な答えを (A) 〜 (C) から選びなさい。

1. What way of serving hamburger is NOT mentioned?

(A) With cheese or bacon (B) With fruit (C) With tomato and lettuce

2. Where do many people believe that hamburgers originally came from?

(A) France (B) Germany (C) St. Louis

3. When did hamburgers first become popular in the U.S.?
(A) In the early 20th century (B) In the mid-20th century (C) In the early 21st century

3 Conversation

A Listen and Write

24

次の会話を聞いて、(　　) に単語を書きなさい。

W: What are your plans for the summer?
M: Actually, I just got a part-time [1](　　　　　　).
W: Really? Where are you working?
M: At a [2](　　　　　　) restaurant. I'm working as a short-order cook.
W: No way. That [3](　　　　　　) like fun!
M: I hope it is. But I'm a [4](　　　　　　) worried. I'm not really that good at cooking.

Notes **short-order cook**「手早く料理をする人」 **no way**「まさか」

B Listen and Choose

25

質問を聞いて、(　　) に単語を書き、最も適切な応答を (A) ～ (C) から選びなさい。

1. (　　　　) (　　　　) the man be (　　　　) (　　　　) the summer?
(A) Checking out fast-food restaurants
(B) Learning how to cook
(C) Working as a cook

2. (　　　　) (　　　　) the man (　　　　)?
(A) He doesn't like fast food.
(B) He is not a very good cook.
(C) He will have to work too hard.

4 Text Completion

次の文章を読んで、空所に入れる最も適切なものを (A) ～ (C) から選びなさい。

Did you know that Americans eat more than 150 hamburgers per person every year? Most Americans make hamburgers __1__ home. If they go out to eat a hamburger, they can choose __2__ among 50,000 hamburger joints, or restaurants. When they do eat out, it is probably on a Saturday, because Saturday __3__ for eating hamburgers at a restaurant.

1. (A) at (B) in (C) to
2. (A) for (B) from (C) with
3. (A) are the day people like (B) have to be the least popular day
(C) is the most popular day

5 Grammar Check

A 空所に最も適切な時を表す前置詞 (at , in, on) を記入しなさい。

1. _____ September　　**2.** _____ three o'clock
3. _____ summer　　**4.** _____ Wednesday afternoon
5. _____ night　　**6.** _____ the weekend
7. _____ my birthday　　**8.** _____ the end of class
9. _____ the evening　　**10.** _____ lunch

B (　　) 内の最も適切な場所を表す前置詞を選び、英文を完成しなさい。

1. My best friend grew up (at / in / on) New Zealand.
2. The restaurant is (at / in / on) the end of the street.
3. The author's name is (of / on / with) the cover of the book.
4. There was a long line of people (at / in / for) the bus stop.
5. The garden (among / beneath / between) the two houses is very beautiful.
6. There's a helicopter hovering (above / on / under) our town.
7. There is a big shopping mall (between / from / near) the station.
8. A small stream runs (across / below / over) the wooden bridge.

C 空所に前置詞 (at, in, on) のいずれかに続く語句を語群より選び、英文を完成しなさい。

~~a day~~	a tablet	Christmas	the countryside	the top floor
time	two hours			

e.g. It's a short story. You can read it <u>in a day</u>.

1. My car is being repaired at the garage. It will be fixed ____________________.
2. Jack doesn't buy many books nowadays. He reads them ____________________.
3. I don't like living in the city. I much prefer to live ____________________.
4. The fancy French restaurant in this building is ____________________.
5. It's impolite to be late. You should come ____________________.
6. Tom goes to his parents' house ____________________ to eat turkey with them.

6 Composition

A 日本語を参考にして、(　　) 内の単語を正しく並べ替え、また [　　] ア～ウに単語を書いて、文章を完成しなさい。

Do you like meat? My ア[　　　　　　] food is the hamburger. When I travel, I 1(always / for / hamburger / interesting / look) restaurants. The hamburger is a very simple sandwich. It is 2(a meat / between / of / made / patty) the two halves of a bun. イ[　　　　　　] though it is so simple, I am always 3(all / by / surprised / ways / the different) people can cook this wonderful ウ[　　　　　　].

あなたは肉が好きですか。私の好きな食べ物はハンバーガーです。私は旅行するとき、いつも面白いハンバーガーレストランを探します。ハンバーガーはとても簡単なサンドイッチです。半分に切った２枚の丸いパンの間にはさんだ肉のパティで作られます。とても簡単ではあるけれども、人々がこの素晴らしい料理を作ることのできる、さまざまな方法すべてにいつも驚かされます。

Word Order:

1.

2.

3.

B 次の質問に、(　　) 内の語句を使って答えなさい。

1. What side dish do you like to eat with a hamburger?

(French fries / salad / clam chowder)

2. What Japanese food do you think visitors from abroad should definitely try?

(katsudon / blend of meat, egg, onion, sauce, and rice)

Grammar Spotlight

▶前置詞

名詞・代名詞の前に置き、時・場所・理由・方法などを表します。

1. 時

I often go swimming **in** summer.
Thomas usually gets up **at** 7 o'clock.
Beth works **from** 10 a.m. **to** 6 p.m.
Tracy will come home **in** an hour.
Judy will have her birthday party **on** June 18th.
You have to finish the task **by** six.
I've been living here **for** ten years.

☞ tomorrow, yesterday, next, last には前置詞を使いません。

× I went to the department store **on** last Sunday.
○ I went to the department store **last** Sunday.

2. 場所

Our office is **on** the 15th floor.
Alex spent a quiet evening **at** home.
The shopping center is **near** the station.
The little boy sits **between** his mother and father.
The birds are singing **in** the trees.
Jessica lives **in** the house **by** the lake.

3. 理由

Jane cried **for** joy.
I was in bed **with** a cold.

4. 方法・手段

I go to school either **by** bicycle or **on** foot.
Billy ate his noodles **with** chopsticks.

Unit 9
How Are New Words Born?

▶ adjectives / adverbs

言葉は絶えず変化しています。グローバル化の流れの中で、英語の変化は著しく、新しい言葉が生まれる一方、消えていく言葉もあります。どのようにして新しい単語が英語に加えられるのでしょうか。

Warm-up Questions

次の質問に英語で答えなさい。

1. What do you do when you have trouble remembering an English word?
2. How about when you can’t remember a word in Japanese?

1 Vocabulary

英文の空所に入れる最も適切な単語を語群より選び、(A) ～ (G) で答えなさい。

(A) constantly	(B) disappear	(C) entry	(D) estimates
(E) evolved	(F) included	(G) longer	

1. I am so happy! My _____ for the short-story writing contest won first prize.
2. Bombay is no _____ called “Bombay” as it was during colonial times. Now, it is known as Mumbai.
3. Some paleontologists say that modern birds _____ from dinosaurs.
4. One of my friends is _____ taking selfies with her smartphone. She takes hundreds a day.
5. The manager doesn’t know how long we will have to wait in this line, but she _____ that it will be about 45 minutes.
6. Nowadays, batteries are not usually _____ with electronics products. You have to buy them separately.
7. I saw a magician make a woman _____. At first, you could see her, and then, just like that, she was gone!

2 Reading

26

The English language has a huge number of words. An unabridged English dictionary may have as many as 300,000 entries! There are also a lot more words that are not included. In fact, some linguists think that English has over 1 million words.

New words enter English constantly. Other words evolve and change meaning. “Tweet,” for example, is a word that refers to the sound a bird makes, but from 2006 to 2023 it most often meant to send a message on Twitter. In addition to these changing meanings, English loves to borrow words from other languages. Words like cookie, lemon, and penguin originally came from different languages.

The spellings of English words can also be different. Do you like “donuts” or “doughnuts”? Words also disappear from the language. This happens when words gradually fall out of use and are no longer used by many people. This has happened to countless words that were used a long time ago, words like *crapulous* (how you feel when you drink too much alcohol), or VHS (recording tapes people used before DVDs).

Notes **unabridged English dictionary**「英語大辞典」 **most often**「ほとんどの場合」 **in addition to**「〜に加えて」 **fall out of use**「使われなくなる」 **no longer**「もはや〜ない」 ***crapulous***「飲み過ぎて気分が悪い」

Reading Comprehension

A True or False

次の英文が本文の内容と一致する場合は T、一致しない場合は F を選びなさい。

1. The English language often borrows words from other languages. **[T F]**
2. Some words in English have the same meaning but have different spellings. **[T F]**
3. English words sometimes disappear from everyday use. **[T F]**

B Skimming and Scanning

本文の内容について、最も適切な答えを (A) 〜 (C) から選びなさい。

1. How many words do some linguists believe there are in the English language?
(A) 1,000,000 (B) 10,000,000 (C) 100,000,000

2. What was the meaning of “tweet” from 2006 to 2023?
(A) To complain loudly
(B) To send a message on Twitter
(C) The sound a bird makes

3. Before DVDs, which of these did people use to watch movies at home?
(A) A Video Home System (B) Compact Discs (C) Digital Versatile Discs

3 Conversation

A Listen and Write

27

次の会話を聞いて、(　　)に単語を書きなさい。

M: Hey. Do you happen to know the name of the capital city of Nigeria?
W: Why [1](　　　　　　　　) you just google it?
M: I'm [2](　　　　　　　　)? What did you say?
W: You know, google it. Do a [3](　　　　　　　　) on Google to find the name of the capital city of Nigeria.
M: When did Google become a [4](　　　　　　　　) word?
W: Don't ask me! You can google that, too!

Notes **google**「グーグルで検索する」 **don't ask me**「知らないよ」

B Listen and Choose

28

質問を聞いて、(　　)に単語を書き、最も適切な応答を (A) ～ (C) から選びなさい。

1. What does the man (　　　　　　) (　　　　) (　　　　　　)?
(A) How to use Google
(B) The capital city of Nigeria
(C) Who started Google

2. What does the woman (　　　　　　　) (　　　　　　) the man (　　　　)?
(A) Ask someone from Nigeria
(B) Go to the library and look it up
(C) Look for the information on the internet

4 Text Completion

次の文章を読んで、空所に入れる最も適切なものを (A) ～ (C) から選びなさい。

If you know __1__ English grammar and usage well enough, you can use words in creative ways to better express the things you want to say. Did you know that adding the suffix "ish" to a noun can turn it into a useful adjective? When you describe one person, place, or thing using an "ish" adjective, you are saying that that thing is __2__ to another thing. You might say, for example, that a kind of noodle soup you are enjoying in Nigeria is "ramenish" because it __3__ Japanese ramen.

1. (A) base (B) basic (C) basically
2. (A) similar (B) similarly (C) similarity
3. (A) does not taste as good as
(B) looks and tastes like
(C) looks different from

5 Grammar Check

A 空所に（　）内の形容詞を正しく並べかえなさい。

1. an ______________________ book (English / interesting / old)
2. a ______________________ scarf (blue / long / silk)
3. a ______________________ jacket (French / leather / black)
4. a ______________________ house (brick / old / really)
5. a ______________________ sweater (nice / wool / yellow)
6. a ______________________ puppy (long-haired / cute / Scottish)
7. a ______________________ cake (chocolate / delicious / round)
8. a ______________________ car (cool / German / red)

B（　）内の適切な単語を選び、英文を完成しなさい。

1. Mr. Bright always drives his car (careful / carefully).
2. I found this new novel very (interesting / interestingly).
3. Cathy is the most (sensible / sensibly) worker in the office.
4. Simon is eating a (healthy / healthily) dinner at home.
5. Claire played the guitar (perfect / perfectly) in the concert.
6. He goes to the gym (regular / regularly) every evening.
7. Jenny has (curl / curly) blonde hair and blue eyes.
8. What's the matter with Laura? She looks so (sad / sadly).
9. (Recent / Recently), I saw a movie that was based on a famous historical event.
10. This coffee is really hot. Be (careful / carefully) with it.

C 空所に入れる単語を語群より選び、適切な形に変えて、英文を完成しなさい。

beautiful	easy	deep	quiet	quick	terrible	wide

1. The couple spoke ______________ because the baby was sleeping.
2. Maria is shy, so she doesn't make friends ______________.
3. This news is supposed to be a secret, but actually, it is ______________ known.
4. Anthony is ______________ upset about losing his smartphone.
5. Michael adapts ______________ to any difficult or unfamiliar situation.
6. She is ______________ thankful to every one of you.
7. There was long applause because the singer had sung so ______________.

6 Composition

A 日本語を参考にして、(　　) 内の単語を正しく並べ替え、また [　　] ア〜ウに単語を書いて、文章を完成しなさい。

A neologism is a ア[　　　　　　] created word that [1](before / ever / has / no one / used). A neologism is born [2](about / people / something / talk / when) new. This happens a lot イ[　　　　　　] of advances in science and technology. Sometimes a neologism come about when [3](an exact / cannot / remember / someone / word). Some common neologisms ウ[　　　　　　] we use today are cyberspace, workaholic, gremlin, and feminist!

造語は今まで誰も使ったことのない新しく作られた単語です。人々が何か新しいことについて話すときに造語が生まれます。これは、科学技術の進歩のためによく起こります。誰かが正確な単語を思い出せないとき、ときどき造語が生まれます。私たちが今日使用する一般的な造語のいくつかは、サイバースペースやワーカホリック、グレムリン、フェミニストです！

Word Order:

1. ....

2. ....

3. ....

B 次の質問に、(　　) 内の語句を使って答えなさい。

1. How many words are there in the Japanese language?
(not sure / find out by googling)

....

....

....

....

2. Describe something from another country or culture that you think is "Japanese-ish."
(paintings of landscapes / gallery / woodblock prints)

....

....

....

....

Grammar Spotlight

▶形容詞

1. 限定的用法：名詞の前に置き、名詞を修飾してその意味を限定します。

Greg is an **honest** man.
Natalie is wearing a **cute** outfit today.
I want something **cold** to drink.

☞ 名詞が something のように -thing で終わる場合は、形容詞を後ろに置きます。

2. 叙述的用法：動詞の後ろに置き、補語の働きをして名詞を説明します。

This black coat is too **expensive** for me.
＜形容詞が主格補語：S+V+C＞
The news made me **happy**. ＜形容詞が目的格補語：S+V+O+C＞

3. 形容詞の語順

冠詞・代名詞など + **opinion**（主観）→ **size**（サイズ）→ **age**（古さ）→ **shape**（形）→ **color**（色）→ **origin**（出身）→ **material**（素材）→ **purpose**（目的）+ 名詞

I love that **big**, **new**, **red**, **Amercan sports** car.
He carries a **big black-leather** bag.

▶副詞

動詞・形容詞・副詞・文全体を修飾します。

Daniela **always speaks confidently** in public. ＜動詞を修飾＞
I was **very happy** to see Andy. ＜形容詞を修飾＞
The woman spoke **really slowly**. ＜副詞を修飾＞
Fortunately, the experiment succeeded at last. ＜文全体を修飾＞
The young woman was **kind enough** to offer me a seat on the bus.

☞ 副詞の enough が形容詞や副詞を修飾する場合は、後ろに置きます。

副詞の作り方

・形容詞の語尾に -ly
careful → carefully　quick → quickly　slow → slowly

・形容詞の語尾の y を i に変えて -ly
easy → easily　happy → happily　lucky → luckily

・-able, -ible, -le は、語尾の e を取って -y
capable → capably　terrible → terribly　noble → nobly

・副詞と形容詞が同じ形のもの
early, fast, hard, high, late, long, etc.

Unit 10
How Do Colors Make You Feel?

▶conjunctions

私たちの生活の中には様々な「色」が存在します。色によって、明るい気持ちになったり、落ち着いた気持ちになったり、私たちの心理や行動に大きな影響を与えます。どのような色がどんな効果を与えるのか考えてみましょう。

Warm-up Questions

次の質問に英語で答えなさい。

1. How are you feeling today? If you could use a color to describe how you feel, what color would it be?
2. Do you feel different on sunny days from you do on rainy days? Explain.

1 Vocabulary

英文の空所に入れる最も適切な単語を語群より選び、(A) ～ (G) で答えなさい。

(A) advertisements	(B) calm	(C) designers	(D) energized
(E) logos	(F) mood	(G) services	

1. I drink two cups of coffee every morning to make me feel _____ and ready to face the day!
2. Nowadays, convenience stores offer customers many _____ such as sending packages or ordering tickets of all kinds.
3. One of the world's most recognizable _____ is the Nike "swoosh."
4. Some fashion _____ create odd-looking clothes with amazingly complex patterns.
5. Sometimes, my philosophy professor is in a bad _____ and loses his temper.
6. When I want to _____ down and relax, I listen to soft music or take a nice hot bath.
7. I'm getting tired of all the _____ for products and services that pop up on the internet.

2 Reading

29

Colors are not only beautiful, but they are also related to our mood and how we feel. Designers often use colors to affect our mood. Look at the logos and advertisements of fast-food restaurants, for example. How many of those logos and signs are painted in bright red and yellow? Most of them! In fact, these colors actually make us feel hungry. Other companies want us to trust them and feel that their products are safe and reliable; so those companies will often use blue or green to create this safe mood and feeling.

There are two basic types of colors: warm and cool. Warm colors—like red, orange, and yellow—are vibrant. They make us feel energized and positive. On the other hand, the cool colors—blue, green and purple—are more relaxed. They are used in places where we need or want to be calm.

So, the next time you walk into a room, take a look at the colors all around you. How do they make you feel?

Notes **be related to**「～と関連する」 **vibrant**「活気に満ちた」 **on the other hand**「一方」 **the next time**「次に～するときは」 **take a look at**「～を見る」

Reading Comprehension

A True or False

次の英文が本文の内容と一致する場合は T、一致しない場合は F を選びなさい。

1. Seeing different colors can affect how we feel. **[T F]**

2. Restaurants use cool colors to make diners feel that the food is safe to eat. **[T F]**

3. Colors come in three basic kinds: hot, cold, and dark. **[T F]**

B Skimming and Scanning

本文の内容について、最も適切な答えを (A) ～ (C) から選びなさい。

1. What colors can make us feel hungry?

(A) Black and white (B) Green and blue (C) Red and yellow

2. What colors can make us trust a company or its products?

(A) Black and white (B) Green and blue (C) Yellow and red

3. What colors can make you feel calm?

(A) Cool colors (B) Dark colors (C) Warm colors

3 Conversation

A Listen and Write 30

次の会話を聞いて、(　　) に単語を書きなさい。

M: I am thinking of [1](　　　　　　　　　　) my house.
W: Oh, really? What do you want to do?
M: Well, first I want to repaint the [2](　　　　　　　　). I don't care for the grayish walls. They're pretty depressing.
W: How [3](　　　　　　) painting them orange? That will give your kitchen a lot of positive [4](　　　　　　　).
M: That's not a bad idea. Thanks.

Notes　**care for**「～が好きだ」　**grayish**「灰色がかった」　**depressing**「気がめいる」

B Listen and Choose 31

質問を聞いて、(　　) に単語を書き、最も適切な応答を (A) ～ (C) から選びなさい。

1. What does the man (　　　　　) (　　　　) (　　　　)?
　(A) He wants to change houses.
　(B) He wants to change the color of the outside of his house.
　(C) He wants to change the color of the walls in some of the rooms in his house.

2. What (　　　　　　) does the woman (　　　　　　　)?
　(A) Grey　　(B) Orange　　(C) Red

4 Text Completion

次の文章を読んで、空所に入れる最も適切なものを (A) ～ (C) から選びなさい。

A recent study on colors showed that people's favorite color changes depending ___1___ their mood. For example, if the people in the study felt happy, they chose yellow as their favorite color. Subjects who were feeling anxious ___2___ upset chose black. If the people being studied were feeling healthy, they would choose blue. Interestingly, subjects who felt depressed chose dark blue. ___3___

1. (A) as　　(B) for　　(C) on

2. (A) however　　(B) instead　　(C) or

3. (A) Do you prefer warm or cool colors?
　(B) What would your favorite color be today?
　(C) Why are you feeling so blue today?

Notes　**subject**「被験者」　**feel so blue**「そんなに落ち込む」

5 Grammar Check

A (　　) 内の最も適切な単語を選び、英文を完成しなさい。

1. You can't succeed (after / because / unless) you work hard.
2. (As / Once / So) Nick is so kind and friendly, everybody likes him.
3. Paul fell asleep (before / until / while) he was watching TV.
4. Sue has quite a few good friends, (but / for / so) she is not at all lonely.
5. Bill jogs every morning (because / however / thus) he wants to slim down.
6. I haven't seen Joan (before / since / that) she and I graduated from university two years ago.
7. We will go camping at Lake Aberdeen this weekend (if / so / though) the weather is sunny and warm.
8. Lisa was tired, (before / or / so) she went to bed early.
9. Jessica reached the bus stop (after / as / by) the bus had left.
10. (For / Though / Yet) Dave is very busy at the office, he makes sure he spends a lot of time with his children.

B 次の 2 文を、and / but / or のいずれかでつないで 1 文にしなさい。

1. She bought a skirt. She bought a jacket.

2. You must hurry up. You will be late for work.

3. Pamela can play the guitar. She can't play the violin.

4. They went to the amusement park. They had a good time there.

C 2 つの英文が同じ内容になるように、(　　) に適切な単語を書きなさい。

1. Greg isn't very polite. Neither is Jenny.
(　　　　) Greg (　　　　) Jenny (　　　　) very polite.

2. Andy likes helping his friends. So does Peggy.
(　　　　) Andy (　　　　) Peggy (　　　　) helping their friends.

3. You can pay in cash. You can pay with a credit card.
You can pay (　　　　) in cash or with a credit card.

4. The comedian can make people laugh. He can make people cry.
The comedian can (　　　　) only make people laugh, (　　　　) he can (　　　　) make them cry.

6 Composition

A 日本語を参考にして、(　　) 内の単語を正しく並べ替え、また [　　] ア～ウに単語を書いて、文章を完成しなさい。

Colors are important. Colors help us [1](of / something / the meaning / to / understand) quickly and easily. Some [2](all / colors / have / meaning / the same) over the world. Red, for example, tells [3](dangerous / is / something / that / us). Yellow is used to warn us to be[ア] [　　　　　　]. Green is often the color used to represent[イ] [　　　　　　]. White lets us know that something is[ウ] [　　　　　　].

色は重要です。色は私たちが、あるものの意味をすばやく容易に理解する手助けをしてくれます。いくつかの色は世界中で同じ意味を持ちます。例えば、赤は何かが危険であることを伝えます。黄色は私たちに注意を促すために使われます。緑は安全を表すためによく使われる色です。白は何かが清潔だと私たちに知らせます。

Word Order:

1. ……………………………………

2. ……………………………………

3. ……………………………………

B 次の質問に、(　　) 内の語句を使って答えなさい。

1. Describe your favorite outfit and its colors.

(polo shirt / grayish Levis / feel proud and positive)

……………………………………

……………………………………

……………………………………

……………………………………

……………………………………

2. Do you agree that colors can change or affect your mood and the way you feel?

(I think that colors can change / For example,)

……………………………………

……………………………………

……………………………………

……………………………………

……………………………………

Grammar Spotlight

▶接続詞

語と語、句と句、文と文をつなぎます。

1. 等位接続詞：語・句・文を対等に結びます。(and, but, for, nor, or)

Joan likes cooking **and** shopping.
We sat on the table **and** (we) had lunch.
(A + and + B の文では、主語が同じとき B の主語を省略できます。)

He wanted to go abroad, **but** he didn't have enough money.
(A + but / or + B の文では、主語が同じでも B の主語を省略しません。)

2. 相関接続詞：連語で対応する語句をつなぎ、等位接続詞的な働きをします。

both A and B「A も B もどちらも」
Tom likes **both** soccer **and** baseball.

not only A but also B「Aだけでなく B も」
Jane **not only** likes to watch movies **but** she **also** likes to go to see plays.

either A or B「AかBのどちらか」
Either James **or** Susan will go.

neither A nor B「A も B も～ない」
Neither romantic movies **nor** comedies fascinate Samuel.

3. 従属接続詞：文（従属節）を文（主節）につなぐ働きをします。

名詞節を導く（if, that, whether など）
I don't know **if** Sarah will understand how I feel about her.
「～かどうか」＜名詞節＞

副詞節を導く（after, although, as, because, before, if, since, until, when, while など）
If it is sunny tomorrow, we will hold a yard sale.
「もし～なら」＜副詞節＞

Unit 11
What Happens When You See Red?

▶ **pronouns / tag questions**

赤色は、私たちの感情に大きな影響を与えます。赤は太陽のような、力強いアクティブなエネルギーを感じさせ、国旗などにも用いられています。気分を高揚させ、活動的・情熱的に私たちの行動を駆り立てるのです。

Warm-up Questions

次の質問に英語で答えなさい。

1. Blue is the favorite color of 35 percent of people around the world. How about you? What is *your* favorite color?

2. What color do you choose for most of your clothes?

1 Vocabulary

英文の空所に入れる最も適切な単語を語群より選び、(A) 〜 (G) で答えなさい。

(A) decreased	(B) everywhere	(C) engine	(D) indicates
(E) international	(F) objects	(G) prefer	

1. Many people in the U.S. have reported seeing strange _____ in the sky called UFOs that they believe came from outer space.

2. A fever usually _____ that we are sick and should see a doctor.

3. I have two flavors of ice cream, chocolate and vanilla. Which would you _____?

4. Because I have so much homework, my time for playing video games has _____.

5. You can see convenience stores _____ in Tokyo. There is one on almost every corner these days.

6. When I was in elementary school, we visited a fire station and went for a ride in a fire _____.

7. My best friend Shizue works for an _____ IT company that has offices here in Japan as well as in the U.S., South America, and the U.K.

2 Reading

32

Red is used everywhere for all kinds of purposes. You can find red in 77% of the world's flags. Red is the international color for stop. The International Red Cross uses it to stand for help and rescue.

Red means different things in different cultures. In many Asian countries, red means good luck. In the Japanese stock market, red indicates that the price of a stock has gone up. On the other hand, in North America, red means that the price of the stock has decreased.

Red is very easy to see. Red makes us imagine that objects are moving forward, which is why so many fire engines around the world are painted red. It is also why police officers use red-and-blue flashing lights. There are two main kinds of red. Red that has a bit of yellow in it is called *tomato red*. Red made with an orange tint is called *berry red*. Studies show that men prefer tomato reds while women like berry reds.

Notes **International Red Cross**「国際赤十字」 **stand for**「～を表す」 **stock market**「株式市場」 **fire engine**「消防車」 **police officer**「警察官」 **flashing lights**「閃光灯」 **orange tint**「オレンジがかった色」

Reading Comprehension

A True or False

次の英文が本文の内容と一致する場合は T、一致しない場合は F を選びなさい。

1. Not many countries still have red in their national flags. **[T F]**

2. Red is often used in stop signs. **[T F]**

3. Red comes in two main kinds. **[T F]**

B Skimming and Scanning

本文の内容について、最も適切な答えを (A) ～ (C) から選びなさい。

1. What percentage of national flags have red in them?

(A) Seventeen percent (B) Seventy percent (C) Seventy-seven percent

2. In the U.S. stock market, what does a red number indicate?

(A) The price is up. (B) The price is down. (C) The price has remained.

3. Which kind of red do most women prefer?

(A) Berry red (B) Cherry red (C) Tomato red

3 Conversation

A Listen and Write

33

次の会話を聞いて、（　　）に単語を書きなさい。

W: Are you OK? You seem a little red in the face.

M: The truth is, I am really embarrassed.

W: Why? What [1](　　　　　　)?

M: Do you remember [2](　　　　　　) me not to tell Barry about his surprise birthday party this weekend? Well, I met Barry in the cafeteria this afternoon, and, well, we [3](　　　　　　) chatting about our weekend plans and ....

W: Oh no! You [4](　　　　　　), did you?

M: I am so sorry. It just popped out.

Notes　**be embarrassed**「恥ずかしい思いをする」　**pop out**「口から出る」

B Listen and Choose

34

質問を聞いて、（　　）に単語を書き、最も適切な応答を (A) ～ (C) から選びなさい。

1. Why is the man (　　　　) (　　　　) the (　　　　)?

(A) He's embarrassed.　(B) He's exercising.　(C) He's sick.

2. (　　　　) (　　　　) the man (　　　　)?

(A) He forgot to tell Barry something important.

(B) He made plans to have a party for Barry.

(C) He told Barry something that he shouldn't have.

4 Text Completion

次の文章を読んで、空所に入れる最も適切なものを (A) ～ (C) から選びなさい。

__1__ To be "in the red" means to lose or owe money. The opposite is to be "in the black." If you see someone doing something bad, you can say that you caught that person "red-handed." When we "see red," it means that __2__ are angry. If you are "red in the face," it sometimes means that you are __3__ about something, but it can also mean that you have a fever.

1. (A) Red is the most popular color around the globe, isn't it?

(B) There are all kinds of interesting English expressions using red, aren't there?

(C) There are many expressions in English that use black, aren't there?

2. (A) one　(B) we　(C) you

3. (A) embarrassed　(B) embarrassing　(C) embarrassment

5 Grammar Check

A (　　) に適切な人称代名詞を入れて、英文を完成しなさい。

1. A: Do you know Brenda's address?
B: No, but we can email Brenda and ask (　　　　　　).

2. A: What are your friends doing?
B: I think (　　　　　　) are making a poster for the culture festival.

3. A: Have you seen your grandfather?
B: Yes. (　　　　　　) is relaxing in the garden.

4. Excuse (　　　　　　). May (　　　　　　) ask (　　　　　　) a question?

5. William is so nice. (　　　　　　) bought (　　　　　　) wife some flowers for their anniversary.

6. I need those books on the top shelf. Can you get (　　　　　　) for me?

7. I'm sorry. Mr. Doyle is not in the office right now. Would you like to leave (　　　　　　) a message?

B (　　) 内の最も適切な付加疑問を選び、英文を完成しなさい。

1. Kitty went to the concert yesterday, (did they / didn't she / wasn't it)?
2. You are Jordan, (aren't you / is it / isn't he)?
3. Ms. Smith won't tell him the truth, (will he / will she / won't he)?
4. Mr. Elton has been to New York recently, (haven't you / has she / hasn't he)?
5. The vintage Nissan sports car isn't in the garage, (is it / isn't it / won't they)?

C 空所に適切な付加疑問を付けて、英文を完成しなさい。

1. Emily will come to my office tomorrow, ________________?
2. Karen and Nick don't like physics, ________________?
3. Henry can't drive a manual shift, ________________?
4. The children are walking home from school, ________________?
5. George has been to Boston before, ________________?

6 Composition

A 日本語を参考にして、(　　) 内の単語を正しく並べ替え、また [　　] ア～ウに単語を書いて、文章を完成しなさい。

Did you know that the most [1](color / in / is / popular / the world) aqua menthe? It is [2](a tropical / blue-green / color / of / the) sea. The second most popular color is [ア][　　　　　　] proton purple. It [3](a field / is / of / of lavender / the color). The third most popular is [イ][　　　　　　] red. This is the color of [ウ][　　　　　　]. Which of these colors do you think is the most beautiful?

世界で最も人気のある色がアクアミントであることを知っていましたか。それは熱帯の海の青緑色です。２番目に人気のある色はプロトンパープルと呼ばれます。それはラベンダー畑の色です。３番目に人気があるのはオレンジがかった赤色です。これは夕焼けの色です。これらの色の中でどれが最も美しいと思いますか。

Word Order:

1. ....

2. ....

3. ....

B 次の質問に、(　　) 内の語句を使って答えなさい。

1. Which do you prefer, warm colors or cool colors?

(I prefer ... to)

....

....

....

....

....

2. Why do you think so many people around the world choose aqua menthe as their favorite color?

(it reminds them of / calm blue sea / blue sky)

....

....

....

....

....

Grammar Spotlight

▶代名詞

1. 人称代名詞

一人称・二人称・三人称の代名詞を「人称代名詞」と言い、主格・所有格・目的格の働きがあります。

I ran into **my** friends. **They** were going on a hike.
I am Elizabeth. Please call **me** Beth.

2. 指示代名詞

「これ」「それ」「あれ」などの、特定の人やものを指し示す代名詞を指示代名詞と言います。

I bought **a new computer**. **It** has many more functions than my old one.
（前の語句を受ける）
Kelly was promoted, but I didn't know **that**. （前述の文を受ける）

▶付加疑問文

話者が「〜ですよね」と同意を求めたり、念を押したりするときに使う表現です。

肯定文では「〜, 否定＋代名詞＋？」
否定文では「〜, 肯定＋代名詞＋？」

This chocolate parfait is really sweet, **isn't it**? ＜ be 動詞の付加疑問文＞
Sandra doesn't like the bag, **does she**? ＜一般動詞の付加疑問文＞

Unit 12
Do You Have a Green Thumb?

▶comparatives

あなたはガーデニングや家庭菜園を楽しみますか。緑色に触れると心も体もリラックスできる人が多いのはなぜでしょうか。自然を象徴する緑色が、庭に居心地のよさを再現し、穏やかで、やすらぎの空間にしてくれるからです。

Warm-up Questions

次の質問に英語で答えなさい。

1. What vegetables do you dislike?
2. What plants do you have in your home or garden?

1 Vocabulary

英文の空所に入れる最も適切な単語を語群より選び、(A) ～ (G) で答えなさい。

(A) associated	(B) benefit	(C) crowded	(D) participate
(E) planting	(F) provide	(G) rural	

1. Many professional sports stars _____ in volunteer activities to help their communities.
2. One big _____ of learning English is that you can watch, understand, and enjoy movies from many countries.
3. I prefer living in the city to living in a _____ area. There's not much to do in the countryside.
4. I think _____ trees to help the environment sounds like a really good idea.
5. Most parents _____ their children with some money every month so the kids can buy things and go out with their friends.
6. I usually avoid big events where there are a lot of people. I really don't like _____ places.
7. Playing video games used to be _____ with people who were not "cool." But today, almost everyone plays video games, so that is no longer true.

2 Reading

35

Having a garden used to be associated mainly with farmers or people living in rural areas. However, nowadays, more and more city and suburb dwellers are planting gardens at home.

Planting a garden or even raising plants in the house is a hobby that can be shared with everyone in the family. Anyone of any age can participate. What's more, small gardens are an excellent way to relax and connect with nature. As an added benefit, home gardens can provide people with fresh vegetables or herbs.

Home gardens do not have to be large, complicated or difficult. In crowded places such as Singapore, it is common for people to start their own garden on the roof of their house or condo, or even in pots on their balcony.

Notes **be associated mainly with**「主に〜と関連がある」 **what's more**「さらに」 **pot**「植木鉢」

Reading Comprehension

A True or False

次の英文が本文の内容と一致する場合は T、一致しない場合は F を選びなさい。

1. Nowadays, it is still the case that only people living in rural areas can plant a garden. **[T F]**

2. Planting a garden is a hobby that only older people can take part in. **[T F]**

3. Planting a garden requires a lot of space and a lot of time and energy. **[T F]**

B Skimming and Scanning

本文の内容について、最も適切な答えを (A) 〜 (C) から選びなさい。

1. Nowadays, where are more and more people planting gardens?

(A) At home (B) In the countryside (C) On farms

2. What does the passage have to say about small gardens?

(A) They help people to relax and connect with nature.

(B) They provide fresh air in their apartments.

(C) They provide us with extra income.

3. In crowded places, where does the passage say some people start their own gardens?

(A) In a special "green" room in their home

(B) On a nearby farm

(C) On the roof or balcony of their home

3 Conversation

A Listen and Write

36

次の会話を聞いて、(　　) に単語を書きなさい。

W: Oh! That salad looks delicious!
M: Thank you. Actually, 1(　　　　　　) came from my garden.
W: You're kidding! I 2(　　　　　　) you lived in a small apartment.
M: I do, but I started a small garden on my 3(　　　　　　).
W: What are you 4(　　　　　　) there?
M: Let's see ... there's tomatoes, cucumbers, green peppers ... oh, and some basil!

Notes **You're kidding!**「冗談でしょう！」 **Let's see**「ええと」 **green pepper**「ピーマン」 **basil**「バジル」芳香ハーブの **1** 種

B Listen and Choose

37

質問を聞いて、(　　) に単語を書き、最も適切な応答を (A) 〜 (C) から選びなさい。

1. Where did the man's (　　　　　　) (　　　　　　) (　　　　　　)?
(A) A delivery service　　(B) A supermarket　　(C) The man's garden

2. (　　　　) (　　　　) the woman (　　　　　　　　)?
(A) Because the man has a garden
(B) Because the man is serving her a salad
(C) Because the man lives in such a big apartment

4 Text Completion

次の文章を読んで、空所に入れる最も適切なものを (A) 〜 (C) から選びなさい。

Although apartments don't have __1__ space, you can still grow a small garden in them if you choose to. Many plants can grow in small spaces. For example, herbs like mint __2__ popular because they don't require a lot of space. Tomatoes are easy to grow, too. Strawberries can even grow in small boxes! Think about __3__. Then try planting one or two plants that you will really enjoy. It won't be long before you'll have your own garden!

1. (A) many　　(B) much　　(C) several

2. (A) are　　(B) be　　(C) is

3. (A) you like what eating
(B) what do you like to eat
(C) what you like to eat

5 Grammar Check

A 空所に形容詞や副詞の比較級、最上級を書きなさい。

原級	比較級	最上級
e.g. new	newer	newest
1. high	________	________
2. gentle	________	________
3. bright	________	________
4. funny	________	________
5. happily	________	________
6. pretty	________	________
7. quickly	________	________
8. tired	________	________

B （　　）内の最も適切な語句を選び、英文を完成しなさい。

1. This laptop computer runs as (fast / faster / fastest) as that one.
2. Sara goes to the beauty salon (often / more often / most often) than I do.
3. Andrew works (hard / harder / hardest) of all the staff in the office.
4. I am not as (confident / more confident / most confident) as Jason is.
5. Natalie went out of the room as (quiet / quietly / more quietly) as she could.
6. Mr. Thomas speaks (slow / more slowly / slowest) than Mr. Bennett.
7. Peggy bought the (little / less / least) expensive dress that she could find in the boutique.
8. Logan can throw a baseball (far / farther / farthest) than any of his teammates can.

C 空所に入れる適切な単語を語群より選び、比較級か最上級にして書きなさい。

cheap	delicious	early	easy	heavy	lucky	thin

1. Caroline is having trouble carrying her backpack. Hers is much ________ than mine.
2. You look ________ than the last time I saw you. You must have lost a lot of weight.
3. Nicolas is the ________ person I know. He just won the lottery!
4. My bento only cost 300 yen. That stand is the ________ one on this street.
5. Please give me your recipe. This is the ________ pizza I have ever eaten.
6. Maya got an excellent mark on the exam. It was far ________ than she had expected.
7. The sooner you leave, the ________ you will arrive at the airport.

6 Composition

A 日本語を参考にして、(　　)内の単語を正しく並べ替え、また[　　]ア～ウに単語を書いて、文章を完成しなさい。

Do you have any plants in your home or apartment? Many people have indoor plants because they look nice. Indoor plants 1(and / look / make / rooms / warm) inviting. There 2(also health / are / benefits / having / to) indoor plants. Plants 3(and / be / to concentrate / help / you) more creative. Plants can also help ア[　　　　　] stress. They also clean the air and give off イ[　　　　　]. Plants really ウ[　　　　　] make us happier!

あなたの家やアパートに植物はありますか。素敵に見えるので、屋内植物を育てている人はたくさんいます。屋内植物は部屋を温かく魅力的に見せます。屋内植物を置くことには、健康上の恩恵もあります。植物はあなたが集中して、より創造的になる手助けをしてくれます。植物はストレスを減らすのにも役立ちます。それらは空気をきれいにし、酸素も出してくれます。植物は本当に私たちをより幸せにしてくれます！

Word Order:

1.

2.

3.

B (　　)内の形容詞を 1、2、3 は比較級、4、5、6 は最上級にして英文を書きなさい。

Comparative:

1. (funny)

2. (tall)

3. (careful)

Superlative:

4. (heavy)

5. (pretty)

6. (interesting)

Grammar Spotlight

▶比較表現

比較表現は、物事を比較するときに使い、同等比較・比較級・最上級の形があります。

1. 同等比較：「〜と同じくらい・・・」 as ＋形容詞・副詞の原級＋ as

   Karen speaks French **as** **fluently** **as** you speak Spanish.
   Scott is **not as** **studious** **as** his brother Seth.

2. 比較級：「〜よりも・・・」 比較級＋ than

   Betsy cooks **better** **than** her mother does.
   The bike is **more expensive** **than** I thought.

3. 最上級：「〜の中で最も・・・」 the ＋最上級

   Vanessa's design is **the** **best** of all.
   Philip is **the** **most reliable** person I know.

4. 注意すべき比較表現

   (the ＋比較級, the ＋比較級)「・・・すればするほど、ますます〜」
   The **more** I talked with Anne, **the** **more** I liked her.
   (the ＋比較級＋ of the two)「2 つのうちより〜」
   This bag is **the** **cheaper** **of the two**.

比較級・最上級の作り方

	原級	比較級	最上級
＜規則変化＞ ・原級に -er, -est ・語尾が -e は -r, -st ・子音＋ y は y を i にして -er, -est ・短母音＋子音は子音を重ねて -er, -est	fast large easy big	faster larger easier bigger	fastest largest easiest biggest
＜ 2 音節以上の語＞ more, most / less, least	useful	more useful less useful	most useful least useful
＜不規則変化＞	good bad little	better worse less	best worst least

Unit 13
The Word "Puke" in As You Like It

▶relatives

『お気に召すまま』は、機転のきいたセリフやハッピーエンドが心地よい喜劇です。「この世はすべて舞台、男も女もみんな役者にすぎぬ」は、誰でも一度は聞いたことがあるでしょう。洒落たセリフや豊富な語彙が観客の心に響きます。

Warm-up Questions

次の質問に英語で答えなさい。

1. What works by the English playwright William Shakespeare can you name?
2. What movies based on Shakespeare's plays have you seen?

1 Vocabulary

英文の空所に入れる最も適切な単語を語群より選び、(A) ～ (G) で答えなさい。

(A) blockbuster	(B) daily	(C) infant	(D) romance
(E) spit	(F) vomit	(G) widely	

1. My mother says that when I was an _____, I didn't cry as much as most babies do.
2. My favorite movies are stories of love and _____ that have happy endings.
3. Summer is when most _____ movies are released that are expected to make a lot of money.
4. Doctors say that even five or ten minutes of _____ exercise can help keep us fit and healthy.
5. The first time I went for a ride on a boat, I got seasick and had to _____ over the side.
6. The noodle dish I ordered was so hot that I had to _____ it out and drink two glasses of ice-cold water!
7. Today, Haruki Murakami is _____ recognized as Japan's greatest living writer.

2 Reading

38

William Shakespeare was a tremendously popular English playwright of the 16th and 17th centuries. He wrote for the common people, and back then, his plays were like today's summer blockbusters. They had it all—romance, mystery, action, violence, humor—and audiences packed into theaters to see them.

Considering how popular Shakespeare was, it is not surprising that some of the words and phrases in his plays—many of which he coined himself—were soon widely used. In fact, many eventually became part of standard English. One of these words is "puke," which means to violently spit up food when we feel sick or eat something bad.

The word most likely comes from the German word for spit, "spucken." Shakespeare did not invent "puke." But he is thought to be the first writer to use it in English literature. This happened in his great comedy, *As You Like It*, when one of his characters says: "At first the infant, / Mewling and puking in the nurse's arms." Nowadays, "puke" is commonly used in daily conversation. You hear it all the time in songs and movies, and on TV sitcoms.

But keep this little warning in mind: "Puke" is still regarded as a somewhat crude and rude way to say "vomit" or "throw up." These are the better choice of words in "nice" conversation.

Notes **coin**「作る」 **spit up**「吐く」 ***As You Like It***『お気に召すまま』シェイクスピアの喜劇 **character**「登場人物」 **At first the infant, / Mewling and puking in the nurse's arms.**「最初は赤ちゃん／乳母に抱かれて、泣いたり、もどしたり」 **sitcom** = situation comedy「シットコム」ホームコメディ

Reading Comprehension

A True or False

次の英文が本文の内容と一致する場合は T、一致しない場合は F を選びなさい。

1. Shakespeare's plays were not at all popular at the time he wrote them. **[T F]**

2. Shakespeare wrote his plays mostly for kings, queens, and the very rich. **[T F]**

3. Shakespeare invented the word "puke" himself. **[T F]**

B Skimming and Scanning

本文の内容について、最も適切な答えを (A) ～ (C) から選びなさい。

1. Which of these is NOT mentioned as an attraction that Shakespeare's plays had for audiences?

(A) Action　(B) Humor　(C) Music

2. Which English word has the same meaning as "puke"?

(A) To coin　(B) To mewl　(C) To vomit

3. Why does the author say that we should be careful when we use the word "puke"?
(A) It is too old-fashioned.
(B) It may not sound nice.
(C) Its meaning has changed since Shakespeare's day.

3 Conversation

A Listen and Write

39

次の会話を聞いて、(　　)に単語を書きなさい。

W: Have you ever seen *West Side Story*?
M: No, I haven't seen it, but I've heard of it. It's a musical, [1](　　　　　　) it?
W: Yes, it is. It's an adaptation of Shakespeare's play, *Romeo and Juliet*. But it takes [2](　　　　　　) in New York City.
M: That sounds interesting. How is it different from the original?
W: Well, instead of two lovers from different quarreling families, the lovers are from rival gangs. And rather than fight with [3](　　　　　　), everyone does a lot of dancing and [4](　　　　　　).
M: Really? I'd like to see that!

Notes　***West Side Story***『ウエスト・サイド物語』　**adaptation**「改作」

B Listen and Choose

40

質問を聞いて、(　　)に単語を書き、最も適切な応答を (A) ～ (C) から選びなさい。

1. (　　　　) (　　　　) the woman and man (　　　　) (　　　　)?
(A) A book about William Shakespeare
(B) A musical based on a play by Shakespeare
(C) A news story about gangs in New York City

2. In *West Side Story*, (　　　　) (　　　　) (　　　　) the lovers (　　　　) (　　　　)?
(A) two dancing classes　　(B) two quarreling families　　(C) two rival gangs

4 Text Completion

次の文章を読んで、空所に入れる最も適切なものを (A) ～ (C) から選びなさい。

Like *Romeo and Juliet*, *As You Like It* is a story of young love. A young girl, Rosalind, falls in love with a handsome young man __1__ name is Orlando. But the young couple are quickly separated. Orlando is treated __2__ by his uncle and must leave his home. Soon, Rosalind must also leave and runs away to the forest. To survive, __3__ as a man.

1. (A) who　　(B) whose　　(C) whom
2. (A) bad　　(B) badness　　(C) badly

3. (A) she disguises her
   (B) she disguises herself
   (C) she disguises oneself

Notes **fall in love with**「～に恋をする」 **disguise oneself as**「～に変装する」

5 Grammar Check

A (　　) 内の最も適切な語句を選び、英文を完成しなさい。

1. We called our friend (who / whose / whom) lives nearby.
2. She enjoys watching movies (who / whose / which) have happy endings.
3. No teacher will ever show students the questions (whom / whose / that) will be on an exam.
4. We want to take a trip to a place (that / where / when) it is warm.
5. I remember the day (when / where / why) my best friend and I first met.
6. Tell me (that / why / when) you were late for class.
7. The girl (who / which / whom) you met yesterday is my cousin.
8. I know a boy (who / whose / which) brother is a professional soccer player.

B 関係代名詞（who / which）を用いて、2 文を 1 文に書き換えなさい。

e.g. The man is reading a book. The man is my new English teacher.
→ The man <u>who</u> is reading a book is my new English teacher.

1. The house is being sold. The house belonged to my aunt.

2. Do you know the man? The man was waiting in the office.

3. The girl is my sister. The girl is talking on the phone.

C 関係副詞（when / where）を用いて、2 文を 1 文に書き換えなさい。

1. Tell me about the town. You grew up there.

2. I will never forget the day. I first met Carol on that day.

3. That is the shop. I bought this suit there.

6 Composition

A 日本語を参考にして、(　　)内の単語を正しく並べ替え、また [　　] ア～ウに単語を書いて、文章を完成しなさい。

Shakespeare lived over 400 years ago. He is one of [1](English / important / in / people / the most) literature. Shakespeare [2](are / characters / created / unforgettable / who). He wrote plays and [ア] [　　　　　　] that had important themes, [イ] [　　　　　　] true love and ambition. Shakespeare also [3](into / introduced / many / the English / words) language. In fact, many native as well as non-native English speakers all over the world still [ウ] [　　　　　　] those words every day.

シェイクスピアは400年以上前に生きていました。彼は英文学で最も重要な人物の１人です。シェイクスピアは忘れられない登場人物を創作しました。彼は真の愛や野心のような重要なテーマを持つ劇や詩を書きました。シェイクスピアは、英語に多くの単語も導入しました。実際、世界中の多くの英語を母語としない人だけでなく母語とする人も、まだ毎日それらの単語を使っています。

Word Order:

1.

2.

3.

B 次の質問に、(　　)内の語句を使って答えなさい。

1. Do you believe in love at first sight?
(I can be attracted to / simply because …)

2. What kind of people do you like?
(smart and funny / ambitious and considerate)

Grammar Spotlight

▶関係詞

1. 関係代名詞

関係代名詞は「接続詞＋代名詞」の働きをする語で､「名詞を説明する節」と「説明される名詞（先行詞)」を結びつけます。

The boy who lives next door loves to play the guitar. ＜主格＞
I have **a friend whose** father is a doctor. ＜所有格＞
Emma wore **the coat which / that** she bought yesterday. ＜目的格＞

先行詞	主格	所有格	目的格
人	who	whose	whom / who
物・動物	which	whose	which
人・物・動物	that	—	that

2. 関係副詞

関係副詞は「接続詞と副詞」の働きをする語で、「前置詞＋関係代名詞」で言い換えられます。

I remember **the day when** we got married. (= on which) ＜時＞
This is **the place where** Kevin proposed to me. (= in which) ＜場所＞
I don't know **the reason why** Beth is crying. (= for which) ＜理由＞
This is (**the way**) **how** I learned English. (= the way [in which]) ＜方法＞

☞ how の先行詞 the way は通例省略されます。

Unit 14
Hip-hop and A Midsummer Night's Dream

▶ **participles / participle constructions**

『夏の夜の夢』は妖精のいたずらによって、恋人たちが騒動を繰り広げる恋愛喜劇です。ロマンチックで夢幻的な世界が展開されます。今日、ヒップホップ文化と結びつき、ラッパーたちがリズムに合わせて、『夏の夜の夢』の詩を歌います。

Warm-up Questions

次の質問に英語で答えなさい。

1. What do you think of magic and magicians? Are they for real?

2. What ideas of yours have changed since you were in high school?

1 Vocabulary

英文の空所に入れる最も適切な単語を語群より選び、(A) ～ (G) で答えなさい。

(A) arrogantly	(B) attitudes	(C) confident	(D) fancy
(E) addition	(F) particular	(G) lyrics	

1. I really like Italian food. In _____, I'm crazy about lasagna!

2. To me, people's _____ are the most important thing about them. I like people who are positive and thoughtful.

3. One day, I want to go to a _____ party where the guests all wear tuxedos and formal gowns.

4. In _____ to the core curriculum, students may choose to take a variety of elective courses.

5. To succeed, you need to be _____, and truly feel that you can do anything you want.

6. I watched a great documentary about hip-hop, but I had to have subtitles to understand the _____.

7. I really cannot stand people who _____ look down on those who are less fortunate than they are.

2 Reading

41

I'll bet you didn't know that there is a connection between Shakespeare and hip-hop culture. But there is … in a way. In addition to his plays, Shakespeare also wrote a lot of poetry, and some of his words are also used as the lyrics of modern music.

One Shakespearean word, in particular, is often used by many musicians. I'm sure you have seen hip-hop artists dressed in fancy clothes and wearing a lot of sparkling jewelry. Or maybe you have watched them walk arrogantly across the stage or heard them talk about how great they are. That's all part of hip-hop culture. When we talk about this kind of proud, arrogant attitude, we often use the word "swagger." The clothes and jewelry that hip-hop artists use to show their talent and wealth is called "swag."

Both "swagger" and "swag" come from Shakespeare's comedy, *A Midsummer Night's Dream*. The words are used in the play to describe confident people and the items they use to show off, as in this famous line: "What hempen homespuns have we *swaggering* here, / So near the cradle of the fairy queen?"

Notes **I'll bet**「きっと～」 **hip-hop culture**「ヒップホップ文化」1970年代にニューヨークで誕生した音楽文化 **in particular**「特に」 **sparkling**「キラキラした」 **show off**「見せびらかす」 **line**「セリフ」 **What hempen homespuns have we *swaggering* here, / So near the cradle of the fairy queen?**「なんとまあ粗末な田舎者どもが、こんなところで大見えを切っているんだ／妖精の女王様のゆりかごのすぐ側だというのに」

Reading Comprehension

A True or False

次の英文が本文の内容と一致する場合は T、一致しない場合は F を選びなさい。

1. Modern musicians sometimes use words from Shakespeare's poetry. **[T F]**

2. Some hip-hop musicians like to show off their fancy clothes and jewelry. **[T F]**

3. "Swagger" is an attitude that is part of the culture of hip-hop. **[T F]**

B Skimming and Scanning

本文の内容について、最も適切な答えや語句を (A) ～ (C) から選びなさい。

1. What kind of people "swagger"?
(A) People who are arrogant and proud
(B) People who listen to hip-hop
(C) People who read Shakespeare

2. Why do some people wear "swag"?
(A) To show that they are musicians
(B) To show that they like Shakespeare
(C) To show their wealth

3. In the quote, "hempen homespuns" refers to someone who is from a low social position. The person in the play is "swaggering," which means that he is _____.
   (A) acting as if he were a musician
   (B) acting as if he were an important person
   (C) acting as if he were from the countryside

3 Conversation

A Listen and Write 42

次の会話を聞いて、(　　) に単語を書きなさい。

W: Have you [1](　　　　　　) our new teacher?
M: Do you [2](　　　　　　) Mr. Shepherd, the English teacher?
W: Yes! He is to die for, if you ask me.
M: Are you [3](　　　　　　)? He has a little too much swag for me.
W: But that's why he is so [4](　　　　　　)!

Notes **to die for**「(死んでもいいくらい) すてきな」 **have a little too much**「少し～過ぎる」

B Listen and Choose 43

質問を聞いて、(　　) に単語を書き、最も適切な応答を (A) ～ (C) から選びなさい。

1. (　　　　) does the woman (　　　　　) (　　　　) Mr. Shepherd?
   (A) He is attractive. (B) He is dangerous. (C) He is too proud.
2. (　　　　) does the man (　　　　　) (　　　　) (　　　　) new teacher?
   (A) He is attractive. (B) He is dangerous. (C) He is too proud.

4 Text Completion

次の文章を読んで、空所に入れる最も適切なものを (A) ～ (C) から選びなさい。

In the world of business, the word "swag" is used quite a bit __1__ from the way it is used by hip-hop artists. At business conferences and conventions, companies will often give out free gifts to visitors, small items such as hats, T-shirts, or ballpoint __2__, all with the company logo clearly marked on them. But if you are lucky, you may even be given a sample of an exciting new product. This "marketing strategy" is one technique companies use __3__. These free gifts, by the way, are called—you guessed it: "swag."

1. (A) difference (B) different (C) differently
2. (A) a pen (B) pen (C) pens
3. (A) to get rid of old products
   (B) to promote their business
   (C) to say "thank you" to their best workers

Notes **quite a bit**「かなり」 **marketing strategy**「マーケティング戦略」 **by the way**「ところで」

5 Grammar Check

A (　　) 内の適切な分詞を選び、英文を完成しなさい。

1. I received an email (writing / written) in English.
2. It was the most (exciting / excited) soccer game of the season so far.
3. A lot of cars (making / made) in Japan are exported.
4. Michael gave Mimi a (surprising / surprised) gift for her birthday—a new puppy!
5. Jim was completely (resting / rested) after his long holiday.
6. The meeting was so (boring / bored) that I couldn't help falling asleep.
7. Olivia was so (embarrassing / embarrassed) that her face turned beet red.

B 同じ内容になるように現在分詞 (-ing) を用いて、空所に語句を書きなさい。

e.g. Did you see the book which was lying on the table?
Did you see the book lying on the table?

1. Do you know the student who is waiting at the library counter?
Do you know ____________________ at the library counter?

2. My friends who are organizing the event are very diligent.
____________________ the event are very diligent.

3. Hurry up, or you will be late for the flight that is leaving at 10 a.m.
Hurry up, or you will be late for ____________________ at 10 a.m.

4. The condo which is being sold belonged to a relative of mine.
____________________ sold belonged to a relative of mine.

C 同じ内容になるように分詞構文を用いて、空所に語句を書きなさい。

e.g. When I was walking the park, I saw a lot of flowers.
Walking the park, I saw a lot of flowers.

1. Because she felt tired, Donna went to bed early.
____________________, Donna went to bed early.

2. If you turn right, you will see the hot spring resort just up ahead.
____________________, you will see the hot spring resort just up ahead.

3. As the book is written in easy English, it is suitable for beginning learners.
____________________, the book is suitable for beginning learners.

4. While I was driving on the freeway, I saw Mt. Rainier far off to the left.
____________________, I saw Mt. Rainier far off to the left.

5. As it was sunny, we went on a hike with some friends.
____________________, we went on a hike with some friends.

6 Composition

A 日本語を参考にして、(　　) 内の単語を正しく並べ替え、また [　　] ア〜ウに単語を書いて、文章を完成しなさい。

Shakespeare's *A Midsummer Night's Dream* is also a [ア][　　　　　　] about love. However, [イ][　　　　　　] *As You Like It* is about young love [1](at / and / first / love / sight), *A Midsummer Night's Dream* is about [2](can / change / how / love / over) time. Real love, in *A Midsummer Night's Dream*, is about [3](more / see / than / we / what) on the surface. It is also about the fairies and fairy [ウ][　　　　　　] that are working behind the scenes.

シェイクスピアの『夏の夜の夢』も愛についての劇です。しかし『お気に召すまま』が若い愛と一目惚れについてであるのに対し、『夏の夜の夢』は時間が経つにつれて愛がどのように変わるかについてです。『夏の夜の夢』における本当の愛は、私たちが表面で見る以上のものについてです。舞台裏で活動している妖精と妖精の魔法についてでもあります。

Word Order:

1. ……………………………………

2. ……………………………………

3. ……………………………………

B 次の質問に、(　　) 内の語句を使って答えなさい。

1. If you could have a superpower, what would it be?
(if I could have / I would like to have the ability)

2. What do you think of people who wear expensive, "name-brand" clothing?
(I like to see / it means that …)

Grammar Spotlight

▶分詞

分詞は名詞を修飾する働きと、補語になる働きがあります。

1. 名詞を修飾

現在分詞（-ing）「～している」

Jessica gave an **inspiring** **speech**.

I know **the man** **walking** over there.

過去分詞（-ed）「～された」

I want **a bag** **made** in Italy.

We learned all about **the books** **written** in old English.

2. 補語

分詞が主語の動作・状態を説明

These instructions are really **confusing**.

Julia was **bored** with the lecture.

Eric was **satisfied** with the test result.

▶分詞構文

分詞構文は、現在分詞（-ing）、過去分詞（-ed）が接続詞と動詞を兼ねた働きをします。

1. 時 「～している間に」

Walking through the park, I saw a lot of flowers.

= **When I was walking** through the park, I saw a lot of flowers.

2. 原因・理由「～したので」

Finishing his work for the day, he went home.

= **As he had finished** his work for the day, he went home.

3. 付帯状況「～しながら」

Carter sat on the sofa, **playing** a video game.

= Carter sat on the sofa **and played** a video game.

4. 条件「～なら」

Turning to the left, you will find the stadium.

= **If you turn** to the left, you will find the stadium.

5. 譲歩「～けれども」

Even wearing a down jacket, I feel cold.

= **Even though I am wearing** a down jacket, I feel cold.

Unit 15
Shakespeare's Unusual Talent

▶discourse / subjunctive

シェイクスピアは膨大な数の単語を作り、自在に使いこなしました。そして観客を言葉遊びの渦に巻き込みました。現代英語はシェイクスピアの英語が基になっています。どのようにして語彙を増やせるのかを考えてみましょう。

Warm-up Questions

次の質問に英語で答えなさい。

1. What do you think Shakespeare's "unusual" talent might have been?

2. What are the opposites of these words? Write them in the parentheses.

1. comfortable	(　　　　　　)	4. kind	(　　　　　　)
2. friendly	(　　　　　　)	5. lock	(　　　　　　)
3. happy	(　　　　　　)	6. well	(　　　　　　)

1 Vocabulary

英文の空所に入れる最も適切な単語を語群より選び、(A) ～ (G) で答えなさい。

(A) adjective	(B) adverb	(C) blocks	(D) especially
(E) noun	(F) similar	(G) verbs	

1. I often listen to American music, _____ hip-hop and R&B, which I really love.

2. An _____ tells us how something is done: quickly, slowly, or carefully, for example.

3. Some words, like book and test, can be both a verb and a _____, depending on how they are used.

4. When I was a child, I liked to play with _____ of all kinds. I used them to make buildings and castles.

5. Adverbs are used to describe, that is, to modify, _____, adjectives, or other adverbs.

6. An _____ tells us what a noun is or looks like—whether it's big, small, yellow, or cute.

7. A simile is a figure of speech that compares two things that are _____ in some way.

2 Reading

44

One reason that Shakespeare is such an important figure in English literature is that he had an unusual talent. He could create, that is, invent and coin, new words and phrases, many of which are now in the dictionary. How did he do this? He (sort of magically) put the different parts of words together like Lego bricks, those little plastic blocks that kids use to make all kinds of cool things.

For a moment, let's think of words as being similar to Legos. The main "brick"—the main part of the word—is called a stem. Other bricks, known as suffixes, can be added to the end of the stem. Suffixes change how words work. Add a suffix to a noun, and it can become a verb. Add a suffix to an adjective, and—presto!—it turns into an adverb.

We can also add other "bricks"—called prefixes—to the front of the stem word. Prefixes change words' meanings. I'm sure you already know lots of great prefixes, such as "uni" (meaning "one"), "bi" (meaning "two"), and "co" (meaning "with").

The more familiar you become with suffixes and prefixes, the easier you will find it to learn, understand, and memorize any new words you come across. Better yet, the better able you will be to communicate your thoughts and feelings. You may even be able to create a word or two of your own, just like William Shakespeare.

Notes **put ... together**「～を組み合わせる」 **Lego brick**「レゴブロック」ブロック玩具 **stem**「語幹」 **suffix**「接尾辞」 **presto**「あら不思議、はいっ」マジシャンの掛け声 **prefix**「接頭辞」 **the more familiar..., the easier**「～をよく知っていればいるほど、ますます容易に」 **better yet**「もっと良いことに」

Reading Comprehension

A True or False

次の英文が本文の内容と一致する場合は T、一致しない場合は F を選びなさい。

1. Lego bricks are toy blocks that kids use to make many different things. [T F]

2. According to the passage, English words are like plastic blocks. [T F]

3. Adding a suffix to a word completely changes its meaning to its antonym or opposite. [T F]

B Skimming and Scanning

本文の内容について、最も適切な答えや語句を (A) ～ (C) から選びなさい。

1. What is the "main" part of a word called?

(A) The prefix (B) The stem (C) The suffix

2. Adding a prefix to a word changes _____.

(A) how the word works (B) the word's origin (C) what the word means

3. Which of these prefixes means “with”?

(A) Bi-　　(B) Co-　　(C) Uni-

3 Conversation

A Listen and Write

45

次の会話を聞いて、(　　)に単語を書きなさい。

M: Hey, Sue. What are you doing?

W: I’m [1] (　　　　　) the crossword puzzle in today’s newspaper.

M: I love puzzles, especially crosswords. Can I [2] (　　　　　) you?

W: Good idea. We can collaborate. What is a six-letter word that [3] (　　　　　) “to open”?

M: I think I’ve got this one. All we have to do is what Shakespeare did and use the prefix “un.”

W: Hmmm ... [4] (　　　　　). Oh! That works! Thanks. As the old saying goes, two heads are better than one.

Notes　**that works**「それでうまくいく」　**old saying**「ことわざ」　**Two heads are better than one.**「3人寄れば文殊の知恵」

B Listen and Choose

46

質問を聞いて、(　　)に単語を書き、最も適切な応答を (A) ～ (C) から選びなさい。

1. (　　　　) (　　　　) the man (　　　　) (　　　　) (　　　　) the woman?

(A) Because he has nothing else to do

(B) Because he loves doing crossword puzzles

(C) Because the woman asked him to

2. (　　　　) the woman (　　　　), “We can collaborate,” (　　　　) (　　　　) she (　　　　)?

(A) That the man should do the puzzle on his own

(B) That she wants to solve the puzzle herself

(C) That they can work on the crossword together

4 Text Completion

次の文章を読んで、空所に入れる最も適切なものを (A) ～ (C) から選びなさい。

One of the __1__ prefixes in English is “un.” Placing an “un” in front of a stem word changes it into the word’s antonym, or opposite meaning. __2__, one antonym for “friendly” is “unfriendly.” So if you needed an antonym for “kind,” all you would have to do is to add “un” to it to make the word “unkind.” __3__ Thus, if you need an antonym for the verb “open,” simply add “un,” which gives you “unopen.” You probably won’t be surprised to learn that the first person to use the “un” prefix was none other than William Shakespeare.

1. (A) most useful (B) much useful (C) usefulest
2. (A) By the way (B) For example (C) In addition
3. (A) The "un" prefix is used to change the meanings of verbs, too.
   (B) Verbs also have antonyms or opposite meanings.
   (C) Verbs, however, cannot be changed by adding "un" to them.

Notes none other than「他ならぬ～」

5 Grammar Check

A "Do you know ～ ?" を用いて、間接話法の英文にしなさい。

e.g. What time is it right now?
→ Do you know what time it is right now?

1. Is there a post office near here?

....

2. Where can I buy a Shinkansen ticket?

....

3. What time does the movie start?

....

B "Can you tell me ～ ?" を用いて、間接話法の英文にしなさい。

e.g. How much is this?
→ Can you tell me how much this is?

1. Is he from America?

....

2. How much does this computer cost?

....

3. What is this device called in English?

....

C (　　) 内の最も適切な語句を選び、仮定法の英文を完成しなさい。

1. It's essential that you (are / be / was) there on time.
2. If Joshua (have / has / had) a vacation, he would visit his grandparents.
3. Emma would take the bus if it (begin / begins / began) to rain.
4. I insisted that Lisa (work / works / worked) on a new project.
5. (If / With / Without) his determination, Jack would not have succeeded in business.
6. We wish you (come / will come / would come) to our office tomorrow morning.
7. If Dave had used his GPS, he would (get / have gotten / not have gotten) lost.
8. Beth talks (as if / how / that) she knew everything about movies.

D 次の各組の英文が同じ内容になるように、(　　)に適語を書きなさい。

1. If I were in your position, I would not do it.
(　　　　)(　　　　) in your position, I would not do it.

2. Robert can't help me because he doesn't have any free time.
(　　　　) Robert (　　　　) some free time, he (　　　　)(　　　　) me.

3. If it had been raining, I would have worn my new rain boots.
(　　　　)(　　　　)(　　　　) raining, I would have worn my new rain boots.

4. As I am not young, I can't walk as fast as Bob.
If I (　　　　) young, I (　　　　)(　　　　) as fast as Bob.

6 Composition

A 日本語を参考にして、(　　)内の単語を正しく並べ替え、また[　　]ア～ウに単語を書いて、文章を完成しなさい。

Shakespeare is [1](amazing / famous / for / his / vocabulary)—for the huge number of words that he knew and used. If you would like to be like Shakespeare, one [2](increase / to / your / vocabulary / way) is to learn a lot of synonyms and antonyms. A synonym is a word that has a [ア][　　　　] meaning. An antonym is a word with an [イ][　　　　] meaning. This [ウ][　　　　] you to remember [3](are / related / that / to / words) each other. For example, one synonym of "big" is "gargantuan," and one of its antonyms is "miniscule." See, you're already becoming a Shakespeare.

シェイクスピアは、驚くべき語彙、つまり彼が知り使用した膨大な語数で有名です。もしシェイクスピアのようになりたいなら、語彙を増やす１つの方法は、たくさんの同意語と反意語を学ぶことです。同意語は、似た意味を持つ単語です。反意語は、反対の意味を持つ単語です。これはお互いに関連のある単語を覚えるのに役立ちます。例えば、"big" の１つの同意語は "gargantuan" で、その反意語の１つは "miniscule" です。ほら、あなたはすでにシェイクスピアになってきています。

Word Order:

1. ....

2. ....

3. ....

B 次の質問に、(　　) 内の語句を使って答えなさい。

1. If you could travel anywhere in the world, where would you like to go? Why?

(I would like to / I have always wanted to)

2. How important is appearance to you?

(judge or decide / by the way you look)

Grammar Spotlight

▶話法

直接話法：話者の発言をそのまま伝えます。

間接話法：人が言ったことを自分の言葉に言い換えて伝えます。

1. 時制の一致

間接話法で主節の動詞が過去形のときに従属節の時制を一致させます。

Peg said, "I **am** going to see the play."
Peg said (that) she **was** going to see the play.

2. 人称代名詞の変化

Tim said to me, "**I** like **your** new coat."
Tim told me (that) **he** liked **my** new coat.

3. 命令文、疑問文の話法の書き換え

Ann said to me, "Please do it at once."
Ann **told** me **to do** it at once.

Al said to me, "Did you go to Broadway? "
Al **asked** me **if [whether] I went** to Broadway.

I asked Liz, "When are you going to Disneyland? "
I **asked** Liz **when she was going** to Disneyland.

▶仮定法

現実にありえないことを「もし～なら、…だろう」「もし～だったら、…だっただろう」という意味で、仮定の状況を述べる表現です。

1. 仮定法現在：現在・未来についての仮定を表し、動詞は原形

She **suggested** that I (should) **go** to the theater.
It is **necessary** that he (should) **apologize** to us.
(that) + S + (should) + 動詞の原形

・提案や要求を表す動詞（advise, ask, demand, insist, require, recommend, request, suggest など）と、要求や必要を表す形容詞（desirable, essential, necessary, important など）に続く that 節内では、動詞は原形になります。

2. 仮定法過去：現在の事実に反することの仮定

If I **had** more time, I **would attend** the rock concert.

・If + S ＋過去形, S + could [would, might, should] ＋動詞の原形

3. 仮定法過去完了：過去の事実に反することの仮定

If I **had had** enough money, I **could have bought** that expensive new car.

・If + S + had ＋過去分詞, S + could [would, might, should] + have ＋過去分詞

4. 仮定法の慣用的表現

Without your advice, I **could not succeed**.
But for his help, we **wouldn't have finished** our project on time.
If it had not been for the traffic jam, I **could have arrived** on time.
He looks **as if** he **knew** the answer to all life's mysteries.

5. 仮定法の倒置

If I were you, I would go to Los Angeles.
= **Were** I you, I would go to Los Angeles.

・If が省略され、were が文頭に置かれます。

If she had arrived earlier, she wouldn't have missed the bus.
= **Had** she arrived earlier, she wouldn't have missed the bus.

・If が省略され、had が文頭に置かれます。

Image Credits

All photographs © Shutterstock.com except:
Unit 5 (p.31) © john j. klaiber jr / Shutterstock.com
Unit 6 (p.37) © Pavel Shchegolev / Shutterstock.com
Unit 13 (p.79) © Robbie Jack / gettyimages.com
Unit 14 (p.85) © Hyoung Chang / gettyimages.com
Unit 15 (p.91) © Oli Scarff / gettyimages.com

著作権法上，無断複写・複製は禁じられています。

Answers to Everyday Questions 1 <High-beginning>

身近な不思議を英語で学ぶ　＜初級＞ [B-958]

1　刷　2024年1月22日

著　者	アーノルド・アラオ	Arnold Arao
	三原　京	Kei Mihara
	巳波　義典	Yoshinori Miwa
	木村　博是	Hiroshi Kimura

発行者　南雲一範　Kazunori Nagumo
発行所　株式会社　南雲堂
〒162-0801　東京都新宿区山吹町361
NAN'UN-DO Co., Ltd.
361 Yamabuki-cho, Shinjuku-ku, Tokyo 162-0801, Japan
振替口座：00160-0-46863
TEL: 03-3268-2311（営業部:学校関係）
03-3268-2384（営業部:書店関係）
03-3268-2387（編集部）
FAX: 03-3269-2486

編集者　加藤　敦

装　丁　Nスタジオ

組　版　Office haru

検　印　省　略

コード　ISBN978-4-523-17958-0　C0082

Printed in Japan

落丁・乱丁，その他不良品がございましたら，お取り替えいたします。

E-mail　nanundo@post.email.ne.jp
URL　https://www.nanun-do.co.jp/